Life Lessons for Loving the Way You Live

Life Lessons for Loving the Way You Live

7 Essential Ingredients for Finding Balance and Serenity

Jack Canfield
Mark Victor Hansen
Jennifer Read Hawthorne

Health Communications, Inc.
Deerfield Beach, Florida

www.hcibooks.com
www.chickensoup.com

We would like to acknowledge the many publishers and individuals who granted us permission to reprint the cited material. (Note: The stories that were written by Jack Canfield, Mark Victor Hansen, or Jennifer Read Hawthorne are not included in this listing.)

Make It So. Reprinted by permission of Christine L. Horner. ©2007 Christine L. Horner.

Seeds of Our Souls. Reprinted by permission of Vicky J. Edmonds. ©2007 Vicky J. Edmonds.

The Light Goes On. Reprinted by permission of Janet Bray Attwood and Chris Attwood. ©2006 Janet Bray Attwood and Chris Attwood.

Confessions of a Goalaholic. Reprinted by permission of Stephen Shapiro and John Wiley & Sons, Inc. ©2007.

Our House, Our Teacher. Reprinted by permission of Michael Murphy. ©2007 Michael Murphy.

(Continued on page 332)

Library of Congress Cataloging-in-Publication Data is available through the Library of Congress.

©2007 John T. Canfield and Hansen and Hansen LLC

ISBN-13: 978-07573-0681-5
ISBN-10: 0-7573-0681-0

Publisher: Health Communications, Inc.
            3201 S.W. 15th Street
            Deerfield Beach, FL 33442–8190

Cover design by Larissa Hise Henoch
Inside formatting by Dawn Von Strolley Grove

*With gratitude
we dedicate this book
to all the teachers
who have given us the
knowledge and wisdom
to love the way we live.*

Contents

Essential Ingredient #1: Finding the Place Where You Belong

Essential Ingredient #2: Filling Your Own Cup

Essential Ingredient #3: Becoming Fearless

Essential Ingredient #4: Holding Hands, Building Bridges

Essential Ingredient #5: To Thine Own Self Be True

Essential Ingredient #6: Getting Beyond Right and Wrong

Essential Ingredient #7: Faith, Grace, and Miracles

Acknowledgments

The authors wish to express their heartfelt gratitude to the following people:

Our family and friends, for their ongoing love and support;

Our publisher, Peter Vegso of Health Communications, Inc., and to all the staff of HCI, for bringing this book to the world;

The staff of Chicken Soup for the Soul Enterprises, especially Patty Aubery, Russ Kamalski, Patty Hansen, D'ette Corona, and Barbara Lomonaco for their guidance and expertise;

Michele Matrisciani, Carol Rosenberg, Andrea Gold, Allison Janse, and Katheline St. Fort, our editors at Health Communications, Inc., for their devotion to excellence;

Terry Burke, Lori Golden, Kelly Maragni, Sean Geary, Patricia McConnell, Kim Weiss, Paola Fernandez-Rana, Christine Zambrano, and Jaron Hunter for doing such an incredible job supporting our books;

Tom Sand, Claude Choquette, and Luc Jutras, who manage year after year to get our books transferred into thirty-six languages around the world;

Larissa Hise Henoch and Andrea Perrine Brower for their talent, creativity, and unrelenting patience while producing book covers and inside designs that capture the essence of Chicken Soup.

Lilli Botchis, for her significant and substantial contribution, energy, clarity, inspiration, and love of this work;

Janet Sussman, for her loving support and guidance;

Bryan Aubrey, for his outstanding editing contributions.

Cindy Buck and Elinor Hall, for their soulful support and insights; and

To the men and women whose stories fill these pages, from whom we learn so much.

We are grateful for you all.

Introduction

Loving the way we live is the closest thing to happiness we've found. The word "happiness" has taken on such a superficial meaning in our culture that it's often used to mean "anything that brings you pleasure." But we have found that true happiness is a quality that emerges and matures in the process of human development. It is closely aligned with equanimity—the ability to maintain your balance in the face of even the most trying circumstances.

This book is about how to experience balance and serenity despite life's circumstances. Like many of you, we have been married and divorced. We balance families and careers. We've survived teenagers in the house—and are wiser for the lessons they've taught us. We've been rich and poor. We've been scared and confident. We love what we do—but didn't always. And we've learned that the greatest contribution we can offer to the world is to live honestly, with integrity, and to be at peace ourselves.

How do we do that? By realizing that we have no control over the circumstances of life, only our attitude toward them. Victor Frankl, who survived a concentration camp by finding the good in everyone—including his captors—

described what we are talking about this way: "Everything can be taken from a man but one thing, the last of the human freedoms: to choose one's attitude in any given set of circumstances, to choose one's own way."

This book is a collection of some of the most important life lessons we've learned to help us adjust our attitudes, find greater balance, and experience the serenity that comes from doing and being our best—no matter what the outcome. In this book you'll find the following sections:

"Finding the Place Where You Belong" is about feeling at home with yourself in the world. "Place" in this context is not so much about finding your right geography, but finding your right work and expression for your creative gifts. The life lessons in this chapter are about feeling natural, comfortable, and inspired.

"Filling Your Own Cup" is about ending the search for things outside ourselves to make us feel happy and whole. It's about tending to our bodies, minds, and spirits, so that we can bring wholeness to our relationships and everything we do—and taking responsibility for ourselves, rather than expecting someone else to be responsible for us.

"Becoming Fearless" addresses how to garner courage in times of fear. This chapter includes stories of survival and new perspectives. Helen Keller may have been right when she said about fear, "The only way out is through." But these life lessons offer tools to help us face worries, problems, and concerns, things like self-trust, heart, surrender, and presence.

The life lessons in "Holding Hands, Building Bridges" offer insights into some of the simplest, yet most significant, ways we can make a difference—in our homes, at work, in the world. From the smallest to the grandest gesture, the experiences shared here illustrate the potential for influence that each of us has.

"To Thine Own Self Be True" takes a close look at what it really means to be honest. Most of us think of ourselves as honest people, and yet, so often we subjugate our voices and our own needs to those of others. This chapter offers new ways of examining our lives and the chance to discover where our outer lives line up with our inner values and where they don't.

The major theme of "Getting Beyond Right and Wrong" is gaining freedom through acceptance and the release of judgments. It's about the world as our mirror and how every person, situation, and event that enters our lives is an opportunity for self-discovery.

Finally, we are so touched by the blessings in our own lives that we have devoted a chapter to "Faith, Grace, and Miracles." The life lessons here direct us to gratitude and wonder, an important part of loving the way we live.

The philosopher Seneca said, "As long as you live, keep learning how to live." That's what this book is about. Each life lesson is followed by a story that expresses the essence of the lesson. (Please note that whenever a life lesson is written in first person, it is Jennifer's telling of her own personal experiences.) Following each story is a section where you may choose to Pause and Reflect, considering how the life lesson applies to your own life and, in some cases, doing something to integrate the lesson into your life more deeply.

While it is doubtful that anyone is "happy" all the time, the ability to accept life's ups and downs provides a platform for ongoing inner balance and serenity. It is our deepest hope that reading this book will inspire you and help you re-perceive your own life in positive ways. For we wholeheartedly agree with the words of Dr. Joyce Brothers, who said, "When you come right down to it, the secret of having it all is loving it all."

—Jennifer Read Hawthorne

Essential Ingredient #1

FINDING THE PLACE
WHERE YOU BELONG

The universe is holding its breath . . .
Waiting for you to take your place.

Jean Houston

LIFE LESSON #1:
TRUST YOUR VISION

If you have built castles in the air, your work
need not be lost; that is where they should be.
Now put the foundations under them.

HENRY DAVID THOREAU

A vision is something that has been seen. It may be a fantasy you had at a young age that you never let go, or a passion that emerged in a time of crisis. It might be born when you find yourself at a crossroads, no longer willing to do things the same old way. It may arise out of need, as an answer to a problem, or a deep soul desire felt within. And it may seem impractical—even impossible.

But remember what the Queen said when Alice in Wonderland noted that one can't believe in impossible things: "I dare say you haven't had much practice. When I was your age, I always did it for half an hour a day. Why, sometimes I've believed as many as six impossible things before breakfast."

It seems to be a quirk of nature that visions can take on a life of their own and find the support they need to come to fruition, once you're clear. If you just trust your vision, the means of fulfilling it seem to gather round in support.

A great example is internationally known hair stylist and

product developer Jon English. Jon's impossible vision came in his early teens, as he was growing up in a rough area of London. His family was so poor that his father always cut his hair for him. Until the day, that is, when at thirteen, Jon put his foot down and ran away from his father as he tried to catch him. His dad finally gave up, tossed him some money, and told him to go to the village for a haircut.

Jon did, and his first "professional" cut at the barber shop changed him forever. As he walked home, he couldn't stop looking at himself in the glass of the shop windows, unable to believe it was really him. He was acutely aware of how his new look made him feel. And in an instant, a vision of giving that feeling to others arose in him. He got a job at a local beauty salon sweeping up hair after clients' cuts, and the rest, as they say, is history.

My vision began to emerge the day I finally admitted that, while I had once loved my job leading business-writing seminars, standing in front of corporate managers from 8:00 to 5:00 had gotten old. So I sat down one day and asked myself what I really wanted to do with my life. The answer came quickly and easily: I wanted to speak—not about how to write a better business letter, but about how to live a better life. I wrote down my vision.

Shortly after that, my dear friend and colleague Marci Shimoff saw the flyer I had created for my new speaking business and asked to join me. It felt like a wonderful match, and our partnership was born. The first thing we did was to write down our vision: "To help women understand and experience their inner power and self-worth, so they can create and live their own vision."

We approached Jack Canfield about our vision and asked if we could create a Chicken Soup for the Soul book for women. Jack said yes; we continued to get clearer and clearer about our vision. We wanted to touch the hearts of women around the world! Sixteen months later, *Chicken Soup for the Woman's Soul* became a reality. Within two months, it hit number one on the *New York Times* bestseller list; a million copies had been sold.

When vision comes from the heart and is coupled with the willingness to work, miracles can happen. Marci and I worked extremely hard on that first book. The learning curve was steep and we had to put the book together while still building our speaking business and teaching in the corporate world to earn an income. Even finding days when we were both in town at the same time was challenging. But we knew it was the opportunity of a lifetime. And our visions proved to be important stepping stones along the path of our destiny.

Christine Horner, M.D., author of the story that follows, also demonstrated the power of vision. Her story is a stunning example of how the universe organizes once a vision is clear, and how—as Marci and I found out—this is usually far beyond anything we could ever imagine or plan.

☕ Make It So

....

When I heard the news on October 21, 1998, that President Clinton had signed the Women's Health and Cancer Rights Act into law, I burst into tears and gave my mom in heaven a high five. "We did it, Mom!" I exulted.

It had been a tough five-year battle to get this legislation passed, but it was worth every frustration I had endured. The new law meant that if a woman had to have a mastectomy and desired reconstructive surgery, her insurance company would have to pay for both operations. In the early 1990s, many insurance companies, in a misguided effort to save money, had decided to stop paying for this essential restorative operation. Now coverage would be required, and every patient would have the option to be made physically whole again.

The seeds of this story were planted seven years earlier, in the fall of 1991, when I opened my solo surgery practice in the greater Cincinnati area. My dream of becoming a plastic and reconstructive surgeon had finally materialized, and I was quite fulfilled helping patients with my surgical skills.

One group in particular struck a deep personal chord in me—the women with breast cancer. My mother was one of them.

One day in 1993, a young woman in her thirties who was

scheduled for a double mastectomy asked if I could reconstruct her breasts. When I sent a letter to Indiana Medicaid requesting authorization to perform the reconstructive surgery, a request that formerly had been a mere formality, I received a reply saying that the surgery was "not medically indicated." Thinking it was a mistake, I wrote again, but the Medicaid executive was unrelenting—the surgery was not considered "medically necessary."

I was outraged and decided that, no matter what it took, I would fight this decision. Not because it was a threat to my practice or my personal finances; in fact, I soon realized that the appeals process would require enormous time and almost certain financial loss. But I couldn't let my patient down. I had enormous compassion for what she was facing—removal of her breasts, chemicals that could make her very sick, possible damage to her organs, not to mention possible death. Added to that, a fear of losing her sexual attractiveness. Then a possibility of being made whole again with surgery, only to have that denied.

Armed with stacks of published research showing that women who undergo breast reconstruction suffer far less emotional trauma, I argued my case before a judge a few months later, and I won.

Unfortunately, I was soon shocked to discover that this case did not set a precedent and had no bearing on future cases. That meant I would have to go through the same draining, time-consuming, financially costly, administrative slugfest for every single Medicaid patient who needed breast reconstruction! Worse still, private insurers started jumping on the denial bandwagon, including Blue Cross Blue Shield of Kentucky, which declared that there was no medical need to reconstruct "an organ with no function."

Reading those callous, cold-hearted words, I vowed at that moment that every woman who must have a mastectomy would also have insurance coverage for reconstructive breast surgery.

I knew laws would have to be passed. But how? I had no political experience. I simply knew if I kept following my heart, somehow I could make this happen.

And so began an awe-inspiring, magical, and profoundly spiritual adventure, where everything I needed would just fall into my lap. Random offers of essential help and serendipitous meetings happened so routinely I came to expect them.

For example, I realized at one point that Senator Ted Kennedy should sponsor the bill because of his success in getting healthcare bills through Congress. A week later, at a state medical meeting, a surgeon from Boston walked up to me and said, "I'm operating on Ted Kennedy next week. Do you want me to ask him to sponsor your bill?"

But it was also frustrating and very difficult work, requiring enormous perseverance and strength. At times the challenges seemed insurmountable.

After the Clintons' national healthcare plan failed, it became unlikely that a federal bill would happen. So I enrolled the help of plastic surgeons, breast cancer survivors, and numerous organizations in every state. One by one, state laws began to be passed. Then more dark news arrived—the state successes meant nothing, thanks to a legal loophole. Another law exempted most people from the protection of state healthcare laws.

At that point, the chances of success seemed as miniscule as climbing Mount Everest, shoeless. But then a personal tragedy refueled my resolve. My mother, the vibrant, extraordinary woman who had taught me to reach for the stars, lost her fifteen-year struggle against breast cancer. As I felt my mother's spirit break free with her last breath, I vowed to let nothing stop me from achieving this goal. I dedicated the project, now called the Breast Reconstruction Advocacy Project (BRA Project), to her memory.

My increasing political savvy made me realize it was now time to go straight to the top—I had to meet President Clinton. Within two weeks, I was introduced to a member of the Federal Trade Commission, who said I could accompany him to Washington on one of his regular trips to meet with the president.

On short notice, I had to cancel forty patients and was told I needed to pay $10,000 for the fundraiser dinner to meet the president. Impossible though it seemed, I listened to the persistent voice in my gut. Before I knew it, I was walking into the Mayflower Hotel and, due to another serendipitous event, was placed at the president's table!

President Clinton was as charming as legend describes, and he knew who I was and why I was there. "You're working on legislation about breast cancer, aren't you?" he asked to my astonishment. Later that evening I had my chance to plead my case.

As nervous as Dorothy trembling before the Wizard of Oz, I started talking as fast as I could. He took careful notes and said he'd look into the matter.

Three days later, I was invited to meet with the president again in Cincinnati. This time I leaped in front of him and blocked him like a linebacker. Dorothy was gone, and Xena the Warrior had appeared! No more than six inches away, I said to him, "My mother died of breast cancer, and so did yours. We can make a tribute to our mothers' lives by passing breast reconstruction legislation!" He handed me his business card with the zip code to the Oval Office. I sent information to the White House and he promised to do what he could. Other doors began to open, including meetings with Hillary Clinton, interviews with *Glamour, Ms.,* and *Elle* magazines, and TV and radio appearances. The issue had touched a nerve nationwide.

The legislation was introduced to Congress in 1997, but

stalled for nearly two years. None of the bills passed that it was tagged onto. With only one day left, it looked as if all efforts were coming to nothing, in spite of the divine support I had received.

The next day, while examining a patient, I was interrupted for an urgent phone call. I learned that the bill had passed, tacked onto the budget bill at the last minute!

I shared a tender moment with my mom, letting her know her sacrifice had made a difference—millions of women would now be helped.

But I couldn't stop at this victory. A bigger challenge presented itself—the epidemic of breast cancer. How could I discover the cause, and help protect women from developing it in the first place? After studying hard and unearthing many answers, I was prodded again to take a huge professional leap. I left my plastic surgery practice in 2002 to dedicate my life to teaching people how to become and stay healthy naturally.

What have I learned? That a tremendous, irresistible power rises up when you make a commitment to creating a better world. In my experience, the universe was more than ready to support me—all I needed was a little surrender and a keen ear to hear the guiding messages.

Christine Horner

Pause and Reflect

1. Keep a journal while reading this book. Write down your reflections, your dreams, and things you discover about yourself along the way.
2. Do you have a vision, a dream, or fantasy about something you'd like to accomplish, for yourself, your family, or the world? What step could you take—either the first or the next step—toward bringing it to fruition?

LIFE LESSON #2:
DO WHAT COMES NATURALLY

I never thought to do it as a job.

CHRISTIAN LOUBOUTIN, SHOE DESIGNER

My career as a professional speaker began when I was about seven years old. I'd gather all the children in the neighborhood and make them sit in rows in our driveway so that I could speak to them.

Later, in the eighth grade, I heard that the local 4-H Club had a speaking contest along with its annual livestock grading and sewing competitions. You had to prepare and deliver a four-minute speech on the 4-H pledge. I thought, *How fun! How easy!* So I joined—and won the contest the first time I entered. The following year I won the state competition on the first try. It seemed that speaking in front of groups of people came as naturally to me as breathing.

I did not realize at the time that I was living my passion. I missed it because, as Deva Premal, our friend and internationally known singer, says about recognizing our gifts, ". . . it's usually right in front of our eyes—that's why we miss it!" Deva grew up in Germany in a home filled with music. She was even trained to play classical violin and piano as a child, but never felt the joy in music until she discovered her own style and genre as an adult. As she points out, society teaches us to appreciate only the things we have achieved through effort and hard work, so it can be easy to ignore the value of what comes naturally to us. So easy, in fact, that for most people, childhood passions never get the chance to become part of their adulthood reality.

In my case, for example, although I majored in journalism with a minor in speech and broadcasting, I very quickly got off track. I got so far away from what I do naturally that I actually spent ten years in the field of accounting. Oh, yes, there were aspects of it that I loved: an accounting system demands accountability, orderliness, and balance, all of which I enjoy. But one day I woke up and thought, *What am I doing?* I was bored. I was uninspired. I felt as if life was passing me by.

I began to reflect on the things I had loved doing when I was younger. I remembered the contests. I remembered being the only student who took speech *as an elective* every semester for four years in high school. One step at a time, I made my way back into the world of communication, eventually forming my own speaking company. I've been speaking happily ever since.

But I'm one of the lucky ones. Eighty percent of Americans do not like what they do for a living. If you are one of them, you are probably spending almost a third of your life doing something that does not bring you joy or satisfaction.

So many of us don't seem to realize that we are each born with our own unique nature, drawn naturally to express ourselves in certain ways. Deva points out that the animals and plants give us such a great example of this: "I've never seen a bird trying to be more beautiful or trying to sing a song more challenging than the one it's been blessed with."

And as Vicky Edmonds would discover, what she does as naturally as breathing now impacts the lives of thousands.

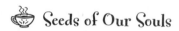 Seeds of Our Souls

My family was poor and my father so abusive I didn't expect to live to eighteen. He once told us he would kill us and hide our bodies, and no one would even notice we were gone. I tried to convince my mother to leave him, but she said, "If I leave, he'll kill us all." I said, "He's going to anyway. Wouldn't you rather die trying?"

She did leave him, and we did survive. But I grew up feeling very small.

That changed in 1988 when, as an adult, I managed to become the "somebody" in my "somebody should do something" cry for help for children ravaged by Hurricane Gilbert in Jamaica. Bringing food to those children gave me courage for the first time in my life. (See Essential Ingredient #4, Life Lesson #2.)

Shortly after returning home from Jamaica, I got the courage to publish my first book of poetry. I had been writing poems since I was eleven, trying to survive my own hurricanes. In my family, children weren't allowed to have thoughts or feelings, and we were not allowed to tell what went on in our house. So mine spilled out onto paper, and writing became my lifeline.

I had written at least 8,000 poems up to this point, and until then I had almost never dared to share any of them, not even with my husband, Ken. So, perhaps it's not surprising that my first book, *Inside Voices,* was about being barely able to open my mouth. I got the courage by thinking, *Maybe if I break the silence it will change the way future generations in my family are treated.*

Part of my fear was that no one would want to read my poems, but my deeper fear was of my family's anger. And, in fact, some of them were furious. My aunts saw a segment on local TV called "If Words Could Kill" that featured my poem "Cutting Room Floor," about trying to edit the abusive words from my psyche. They told my mom I was telling lies about the family. I learned from my mother that none of them had known the extent to which my father had abused us. Ironically, the event brought my mother closer to her sisters. She told them the truth and got to be comforted for the first time.

Realizing that trying to keep the secrets was killing me,

I published my second book of poetry a year later, titled *used to the dark*. It was an even deeper surgery on my pain and isolation. I donated some copies to a project called Books for Prisoners and a few weeks later got a call from a woman working at the local juvenile prison. She said she had a group of girls she had been trying to reach, but nothing had been happening "except attitude." Then she read the girls my poems. "They get really quiet and then just fall open," she said. "Suddenly they're saying, 'That happened to me!'" My writings had given them permission to break their silence.

When she asked me to give a reading at the prison, I asked if I could give a poetry class at no charge instead. After writing with those girls for twelve weeks I made a book of their writings called *Confinement: The Things We Keep Locked Up Inside*. Many of the poems explored an idea I had given them: If you lock up your secrets and your thoughts of worthlessness, you can't see through them to your good qualities. If you hide the parts you think are ugly, you don't let yourself see your beauty.

I gave copies of the book to a treatment center for kids with drug and behavioral problems. One thing led to another, and I've been giving poetry classes there for the last thirteen years. In fact, I've worked with hundreds of thousands of adults and children now: battered women, prisoners, gang kids, sex offenders.

One of my most amazing experiences was at a community center where gang and street kids aged twelve to twenty would come on Fridays and Saturdays between 10:00 PM and 2:00 AM to get food, play board games, and shoot hoops. The kids had to check their guns and knives at the door with an off-duty police officer. They knew they wouldn't get their weapons back, but they came anyway. The youth crime rate went down 53 percent in the neighborhood while this program was operating. I was brought in as part of the high-school general equivalency diploma (GED) program, expecting six or seven kids. But at times we had as many as twenty-eight kids sitting on each other's laps, writing poetry. I published their poetry in a book they named *Lost Between the Cracks*—because they felt they were "throwaway kids."

Over time I found it wasn't just the gang kids who had painful secrets. A group of eighth-graders at my son's middle school wrote poems I published for them in *Between the Lines: Things We Still Can't Say Out Loud*. Even at this middle-class school, I found the same sense of worthlessness—which I regard as the biggest lie ever told. I feel that if I can get the kids to consider that it's a lie, they can look for the ideas and the seeds they hold inside.

My own boys are growing up healthy, whole, and self-confident. Lucas is now a hip-hop artist (L-Agua) who composes amazing music and lyrics. He produced an album with his best friend for their senior project in high school. Ean doesn't like to sit down long enough to write anything, but when he does, it's wonderful. A poem he wrote in middle school begins: "Knowing we two would be the same, I looked for you in the places I would be."

For me, everything started when I had the thought, *I wish somebody would do something,* and answered it with the question, *Could I be somebody?* I went from believing I had nothing to give to seeing that I could feed hundreds of Jamaican children. Now there aren't enough days in the year to give all the gifts I have to give. When I work with adults and kids, I try to prove to them that they, too, are somebody, and they, too, have boundless gifts to give. I tell everyone I work with, "You cannot prove your worthlessness to me."

We all have inside us delicious food and medicine that the world desperately needs. Every single person I see now, I wonder, *What medicine is hiding inside them? What food is waiting there to be given to us all?* To be an instrument through which these things can be revealed goes way beyond joy. It is as essential for me as breath.

Vicky Edmonds

Pause and Reflect

1. Make a list of six things you do well and that come naturally to you. In an average day, how many of these things do you get to do?
2. Does your work provide you with opportunities to do the things you do best? Think of several ways in which you could gradually incorporate more of these activities into your daily routine.
3. What are you here for? Ask your heart, then write it down.

LIFE LESSON #3:
READ THE SIGNPOSTS

You have to trust your inner knowing. If you
have a clear mind . . . you won't have to search
for direction. Direction will come to you.

PHIL JACKSON

I recently asked my twenty-something son if he was dating. He said, "No, I'm looking for someone who inspires me!" Ah, if all of life could be based on inspiration—our relationships, our work, exercising, eating right.

Do you know what inspires you? Reading the signposts of inspiration is a wonderful way to discover the place where you belong. It's especially useful if you can't remember what you were naturally drawn to as a child— let alone make any connection whatsoever between childhood loves and your present-day reality.

Signposts are simply your own reactions to the people, events, situations, music, books, television shows, movies—anything and everything that shows up in your life. They serve as an auto-feedback loop that practically shouts when enthusiasm, joy, or inspiration are present.

Let's say you're a huge *American Idol* fan. Why? Do these young men and women inspire you because they're so gutsy? Or do you love the feeling you have when someone succeeds? Would you like to feel that about yourself?

Let's say you get five brochures a week on public seminars coming to your area—and you decide to register for one of them. Why? Is the topic something that's interested you forever? This could be the first step on a new career path.

What makes you subscribe to an online newsletter? I only subscribe to two, and one of them is all about words—practically my favorite thing in life! The other is about two musicians I love and whose newsletter is soft and informative—looking at it just makes me feel good.

Whom do you admire at the place you work? Why do you love going to your kid's soccer games? When you're channel surfing, what catches your attention? Have you ever met someone and thought: *I want to be like her?*

Janet Attwood, author of the next story, knows all about inspiration. She currently makes her living helping others find their true inspiration by paying attention to the signposts in their own lives. Janet's story picks up when she was only eight years old, but let me fill you in on some significant events before and after that point.

When Janet was very young, she and her mother had a love affair going on. They so cherished being with each other that her mother would sometimes come to kindergarten and take her out of class, just so they could spend time together. But by the time Janet was seven, her beloved mother had become an alcoholic. Close to homeless, she wandered from shelter to shelter, frequently living in $4-a-night motel rooms.

By the time she was in her late teens, Janet was a drug addict. She rode with the Oakland Hell's Angels. At seventeen she was sexually abused. Still, she navigated through a life of lost-and-found dreams, never giving up, always paying attention to the signposts.

Janet likes to say that passions are our breadcrumbs, leading us to the next step of our destiny, ultimately bringing us home. Her story describes how she discovers her passion—again and again and again—and how her passions have brought her life full circle.

The Light Goes On

I was only about eight years old at the time. I used to lie in bed at night waiting for everyone in my family to go to sleep.

I would then sneak outside and enter my imaginary world. Underneath the corner street light, I pretended that I was a beautiful, world-famous actress performing to thousands of admirers. Into the quiet of the early morning, I would sing and dance with total abandon, feeling truly alive and free.

Whenever my relatives came to visit, I always made sure Dad had me dance and sing for them, and I longed to attend a nearby dramatic arts school called Pasadena Playhouse. I pleaded with my parents to let me go there, but when my dad finally agreed, my dream had already died.

"I'm too old," I said. Since I was older than Shirley Temple when she started acting, I thought I had waited too long and blown my chance at stardom.

So, in that fateful moment, my fantasy world collapsed, and by the time I turned eighteen I had started living an uninspired version of "real life." I never had a thought about what I loved to do or wanted to do.

When I needed a job, I scanned the classifieds. My only questions were: how hard would I have to work, and what was the pay? In 1981, I started working for a technical recruiting company in San Jose, California, in the heart of Silicon Valley, hunting for "disk drive engineers." My employer was enjoying huge success. There was a bell that rang whenever someone made a placement, and it rang many times each day.

Unfortunately, it never rang for me. I watched placement after placement being made, everyone congratulating everyone else, new cars and houses being bought, wonderful vacations being taken—while I just sat at my desk waiting for the clock to strike five. Every day I left work humiliated, angry, depressed, and broke.

I had been hired by this elite company because almost everyone who worked there was a friend of mine. When a vacancy came up, my friends all agreed it was the perfect job for me. And why not? I was known as a great communicator, a dynamo of energy who could get anything done.

But it never occurred to anyone that I had no "left brain," engineer-like capabilities, and that I wouldn't be able to communicate with prospective engineers.

One day I happened to see a flyer for a motivational course called Yes to Success, and I knew I had to take it.

The course leader was a young woman named Debra who emphasized the importance of "finding your passion."

As I watched Debra presenting ideas like time management and goal setting, I was less interested in what she was saying than in who she was being.

She was clearly living her passion—and it showed in every word and gesture. Debra was a truly happy person, uplifting everyone not only with her profound understanding, but also with the love she radiated. At the same time, she was traveling the world, making money doing what she loved, and doing it brilliantly.

Debra taught us that when we saw a person who had something we wanted, we should move beyond envy and just tell ourselves, *That's for me!*

I took that advice to heart. Closing my eyes, I silently repeated my new mantra: *That's for me! That's for me!*

By a stroke of good fortune, I was able to drive Debra to the airport when the course ended. As we were waiting for her plane, she asked, "What is your dream, Janet?"

I replied, "I'm glad you asked! I was thinking today that you should either hire me or move over, because I am going to be the most successful transformational speaker on the planet."

Just then there was an announcement that the plane was ready for boarding. Without a word, Debra gave me a hug, turned quickly, and walked off. *She hasn't seen the last of me!* I thought, knowing that my days as an uninspired drone were about to end. One thought burned in my mind: *How could I convince Debra to hire me?*

Finally I came up with a plan. In the coming months, Debra would be teaching in New York, Boston, and Washington, D.C. I decided I would fly to every one of those cities and sit in the front row of every class. When Debra saw me she would know I meant business—especially after the third or fourth course. The only thing I needed was enough money for all the expenses involved.

That night I ran into a friend of mine. When she casually asked what I had been doing, I startled her by passionately declaring I had finally discovered my purpose on this planet. I told her about my plan, even though I didn't know how I was going to get the money.

We got together again the following evening. As we were

getting up from meditation, she opened her purse, showered ten crisp $100 bills on my head, and laughingly said, "Merry Christmas!" I sat there with my mouth open. As tears came to my eyes, I thanked her for believing in me and promised that very soon I would repay her generosity.

I attended each of Debra's seminars. Finally, she came up to me and said, "Okay, if I can't get rid of you, I better use you. You're hired!"

I was on my way to my dream, but as I sat through Debra's seminars, time after time, something much more important happened.

Recognizing the fire inside me, I began traveling all over the world helping people discover their own passion. Occasionally I still write and perform songs, mostly for friends, but my childhood dream to be in front of people has found its greatest fulfillment in speaking to thousands of people, from millionaires to the woman next door, helping them discover what inspires them. Thank God I said yes to success!

What touches me most deeply is working with youth detention centers and shelters for the homeless—perhaps it is because I so easily could have been one of them. But every face I see smiling with surprise, or radiating with possibility and hope, is a signpost that I am on the right track—and always have been.

Janet Bray Attwood

Pause and Reflect

1. What or who inspires you, and why? Are you living according to what most inspires you? What was your childhood dream and what happened to it? What changes would you have to make to ensure that what inspires you becomes more of a practical guiding principle in your life?

2. Pay attention this week to the things that claim your interest. Notice if any of these things draw your attention because they inspire you.

Life Lesson #4:
Let Go of Goals

Getting there isn't half the fun—it's all the fun.

ROBERT TOWNSEND

Have you ever noticed that, no matter how hard we try, we cannot control the circumstances of our lives? Were you born into the family you wanted? Do you love the geography where life has taken you? Are you happy in that job you thought was going to be perfect? Did your children turn out the way you would have liked?

Have you noticed that you'll do something to produce a certain result, only to find that the outcome is completely different from what you expected or hoped for? It seems that we can plan, set goals, create visions and master plans, and take steps to achieve them, but we never know how the details and the circumstances of our lives will play out. We never know whether the life we envisioned will dissolve or fade away. Or morph into something completely different, even unimaginable—either for better or for worse.

Despite this understanding and observation of my own life, I've certainly tried making goals and going for them. I've tried setting yearly goals. I've set five-year goals too, and once I even attempted a ten-year plan for my life. I dutifully read over my list of goals twice a day, every day, reading them with great intention and sincere reflection.

Some of them came to pass, others didn't. Some happened quickly, others took thirty years. For some of them I worked hard; they never came to fruition. Others happened almost overnight, with seemingly little effort.

What does this say about goal setting? There's certainly nothing wrong with it. In fact, goals can provide badly needed structure and direction. But our ability to let go of goals is as important as our effort to fulfill them. For example, when my last book was released, I immediately jumped into action to pursue my goal of getting my book "out there." I effected the same kind of massive publicity campaign I had undertaken in prior years for my early Chicken Soup for the Soul books. But after five painful months of traveling and early morning television appearances that left me bleary-eyed, I realized that I had failed to adjust to the reality of a changed climate in the world of publishing, one in which 600 books are published in this country every day. The competition, in other words, was brutal.

I next set my sights on the goal of creating websites— not just one, but two—because I thought that's what was required of a "successful" author in these times. I just kept pouring money and energy I didn't have into "making it happen."

Then one day I woke up and asked myself what might

happen if I let go of these goals. The thought stopped me in my tracks. I couldn't think of what else I might do with my life. I couldn't imagine what that might look like. But deep inside, I felt the warmth of a growing seed of "not knowing." It felt delicious.

That experience reminds me of what my former publicist, Arielle Ford, said about her own life: "The greatest revelation I've had is to live without knowing, and have that be okay. I could not have written a five-year plan for my life and have it turn out the way it has, because it is so much vaster than anything I could have imagined."

The next thing that happened was that I discovered Stephen Shapiro's book on goal-free living. It changed my life and continues to shape the way I live every day. Read on to get his perspective on what happens when we let go of our goals.

Confessions of a Goalaholic

My story starts June 1986, in Ithaca, New York, when I graduated from Cornell University with a degree in industrial engineering. It was a time of possibility and new beginnings. I had a job with one of the top consulting firms in the world and was dating a great woman, Beth Anne. On August 31st of that same year, we were married. Passion ignited my marriage; goals would kill it.

My first major consulting project was in New York City, developing a computer system using new and unproven technology. As expected, this project required long hours. The three-hour round trip commute from Connecticut was unbearable and I often worked from 9:00 AM until 2:00 AM. The company put me up in an apartment in the city to reduce travel time, which meant I only saw Beth Anne on the weekends—if then. I was myopically focused on my work, solving our numerous technical problems, but taking little notice of my looming relationship problems. Achieving success in consulting became my primary objective. My goal was to make partner in this consulting firm even though I knew that wouldn't happen for more than ten years.

Consistently working eighty-plus hours a week, however, left little time for nurturing a new relationship. I was not spending enough time with Beth Anne; my goals took precedence. What's worse, when we were together, I was always tired. After several years, Beth Anne decided we should go our separate ways. She was right. We had grown so far apart that splitting up was the only option. It was very painful, and only after our separation did I realize that my marriage mattered more than my job. But it was too late. I went into a funk. When I emerged, I started to reevaluate my priorities.

I am not certain if my goals drove me to work the crazy hours, or if I used my goals as an excuse to avoid issues in my personal life. I was so wrapped up with work and success that I forgot to have a life. I wondered if this was what I really wanted. Was having a successful career the most important thing in my life?

My immediate reaction was to leave the consulting world to pursue something I really loved—whatever that might be. Instead, I took a less radical route, doing more of the things that I enjoyed, such as playing my saxophone in local bands while keeping my day job. Still, work and chasing the goal of becoming a partner remained my top priorities.

I was whisked off to a project with a major corporation that needed to cut its employee headcount to satisfy shareholder expectations. I was working long hours in a soulless, sterile corporate environment. Our work on this project would result in the loss of 10,000 jobs, a number so big, so impersonal, it was unfathomable. I did not fully grasp the ramifications of our efforts until I saw a news program featuring a story about my client and three of their executives who had recently been let go. One was mowing lawns to make ends meet. He spent most of the interview crying. The second was spending about fifteen hours a day networking as he looked for another job. Although he had been unemployed for over a year, his story was the most upbeat of the three. The third person had committed suicide. The impact on these three layoffs was unacceptable to me. The impact on 10,000? Unconscionable.

Once again, I thought of leaving consulting, but despite this existential crisis, I wasn't ready to sacrifice the safety net of my successful career. To balance both financial security and personal satisfaction, I decided instead to take a two-month leave of absence. I could not continue to do work that could cause such a negative impact on the lives of so many. During my time off, I took personal development classes, read books on Eastern philosophies, and spent days at the beach writing in a journal and thinking about what I should do. After eight weeks of introspection, I knew what I wanted: a career that would inspire me. I wanted something that aligned with my personal values, without the responsibility for the loss of so many jobs. Achieving my goals at the expense of my soul was not worth it.

I started thinking about growth rather than downsizing. Innovation and creativity rather than efficiency. I decided that within five years I wanted to be a leader in innovation and make a positive impact in the business world. I modeled my definition of success after several luminaries. Like them, I wanted to give keynote speeches, do research, write books, conduct training classes, travel, and make a huge and visible impact in the world.

On the advice of friends and colleagues, I developed a plan to achieve this goal. Handwritten, it was several pages long, detailing what I would do next week, next month, next year, and so on, until my goal was achieved. If I chose to follow this plan, I would have to work exceptionally hard at something that did not interest me and take lots of uninspiring classes. I would need to dedicate my life to this goal for the next five years.

Soon after, I had an interesting conversation with a friend who clearly knew me better than I knew myself. She said, "I've noticed that people are asking you to design your future. Do not let them. In my eyes, you are like a frog. You should sun yourself on a lily pad until you get bored. Then, when the time is right, you should jump to a new lily pad and hang out there for a while. Continue this over and over, moving in whatever direction feels right."

Her words resonated. I ripped up my five-year plan. From that moment on, I embraced the concept of living goal-free. I still aspired to be a leader in innovation—not as a goal, but rather as an intention that subconsciously shifted my thoughts, feelings, and actions. Instead of taking the path that my now torn-up plan had so carefully charted, I decided to take an unconventional path.

After several smaller skips, I took my first major leap off the lily pad and moved to London, still working in management consulting. I rented a small, furnished one-bedroom apartment with a month-to-month lease. Living and working in England was an educational, enriching experience. While there, I chose projects of interest rather than those that would help my career. Flash ahead two years—and five years after the declaration of my "aspiration"—when my book *24/7 Innovation* hit the bookstores. That was when I decided to hop onto another lily pad.

I ditched my six-figure consulting job, gave up my apartment, divested myself of my belongings, and began traveling the world. I created a business in which I would give speeches, conduct research, write books and articles, conduct training classes, and make an impact in the business world, much like I had envisioned many years before.

Although in my first year I took a 90 percent pay cut, I truly love my life. Money, status, and traditional success are no longer motivators. I now use a different measure of success, one built on my contribution given rather than on monetary rewards. Despite this detachment from money, the business is thriving and evolving. My book on goal-free living represents another lily-pad hop for me. I have no idea what the future holds, but I do know that I wake up every day energized, excited, and filled with expectations.

Looking back, I realize that for many years I was a goalaholic. My story is typical of many. Goals made me successful, but unfortunately, they provided little passion or satisfaction along the way. I didn't recognize this at the time. It was easy to get caught up in society's definition of success: money, status, and achievement. We are all told this is the best way to live. But now I look at my life in a new way.

Yes, I still have a type-A personality, but I am a goal-free type-A individual. I am committed to following my passion and playing hard in everything I do. It never feels like work. In following my passion, I often end up taking a different path than I originally imagined. Yet I am still successful, and, I am proud to say, goal-free for ten years. My life has never been better.

Stephen M. Shapiro

Pause and Reflect

1. Are you trying too hard to achieve your goals? What might happen if you dropped your timetable for achieving goals?
2. Does that thought make you feel more relaxed, or nervous? Why?
3. If you could create your own perfect day, what would it look like?

LIFE LESSON #5:
TRY SOMETHING DIFFERENT

....

Determine that the thing can and shall be done,
and then we will find the way.

ABRAHAM LINCOLN

Humans tend to be creatures of habit. We like our routines, and often our lives run in well-worn grooves. Of course, there is nothing wrong with indulging in the familiar; it provides a sense of order and security in our lives. But a life of routine can also become predictable and boring. It can cut us off from the wellspring of life and make us unable to respond freshly, in the moment, when new ideas and situations present themselves.

Once in a while it's a good idea to try something different, to go beyond our normal boundaries and comfort zones and take just a little bit of a risk. Someone we know, who had never learned to swim as a child and was afraid of water, decided to try something different when, in his midforties, he plucked up the courage to take swimming lessons. Overcoming his body's resistance to leaving the familiarity of the earth beneath his feet, he discovered the sheer joy of moving through water.

Sometimes we close off new possibilities or pleasures for ourselves by clinging to old, unexamined beliefs. An amusing example of this was a TV ad a few years ago for a well-known beverage. A man drinks a glass of the advertised product, with great enjoyment, but without knowing what he's drinking. When someone informs him, he says with astonishment, "But I hate _____ !" In other words, he had a preconceived idea about what he liked and didn't like, but when he inadvertently tried something different, he found out what he had been missing.

On some occasions we might hear a little voice inside saying, *I'm not even going to consider doing that because it just isn't the kind of thing I do!* Try gently asking that voice, *Why not?* Often, it's just the habit or the fear of not being in control that keeps us from trying something new, or something old in a new way.

Trying something different can help us when we're stuck. As the saying goes, if you keep doing the same thing, you will continue to get the same result. Do you want the same result today that you had yesterday? Sometimes. But sometimes not. Life is always here, right now, with its myriad possibilities in every moment. If we can just once make that decision, *I'm going to try something different,* we will open up pathways within us in which creativity can flourish, unexpected connections can be made, and new possibilities explored.

It certainly worked for Michael Murphy, whose story follows.

☕ Our House, Our Teacher

I read the letter to my wife, Susie, after recovering from my shock. The management was raising our rent by ninety dollars. Our finely tuned budget had just hit a landmine.

Over the next few days a crazy idea kept coming to me. I tried to dismiss it, but it kept coming back: *Build a house.* It was crazy because we had no savings and were both working full-time trying to make ends meet. Gradually though, a strange kind of logic began to assert itself. If we spent the next five years trying to build a house with no resources, we would probably fail—but we might succeed. On the other hand, if we didn't try, we would definitely end up with nothing.

We decided to embark on a grand experiment. We would simply proceed as if the enormous obstacles didn't exist. Believe me when I tell you this was not characteristic of us. I, at least, was one who always saw the obstacles to any proposal, all the ways it could end in disaster. But our feeling of helplessness at the rent increase had driven us into a corner, and we felt compelled to try something different.

I had heard about the value of visualizing what you want for your life. So I started by drawing plans for a large Swiss chalet, and that fall, we spent our weekends looking at land. One Sunday, we stopped at Susie's parents' after looking at a lot nearby. We decided not to tell them our scheme because they were practical Mainers—they'd think we were insane. But as we were leaving, Susie's mom noticed the blueprints on the dashboard of our car. We sheepishly told them what we were doing, and we drove off feeling silly.

A few days later they invited us to dinner. "Bring your house plans," Susie's mother said. After dinner they grilled us about our plans, and we anticipated a lecture about practicality. Instead, they said they were giving us enough money to buy land and pay for the groundwork. We were flabbergasted. Did they know something we didn't? They were offering to start us on a project we had no means of finishing. Still, we figured land is never a bad investment, so we took them up on it. We found a few acres near the Kennebec River that winter.

By the Fourth of July, we had a driveway, a foundation, and a septic system. We had stretched the money enough that we could buy lumber and begin framing on our weekends. Susie and I worked hard, but with a seven-year-old daughter who had to be kept out of harm's way, it was slow going. By late August, though, we had a plywood platform.

Then disaster struck. I was laid off from my job as a typewriter repairman. Finances became tighter still, but it also meant I had much more time to work on the house. Since the job market was depressed, I went full-steam ahead that fall.

By mid-January the money from Susie's parents was gone. We had framed up a good-sized house. Maine went into a deep freeze, and there it stood, our frozen half-baked dream. We couldn't take out a construction loan, because I had no job, and Susie's was only seasonal. Had we built a huge monument to our folly?

In our snug apartment I sat down to confront the neglected paperwork. I had at least separated the bills from the junk mail and credit card offers. Then a second crazy idea occurred to me. We could accept the credit cards, finish the house enough to move in, and then use the money that was now going to rent to pay the cards off. If anything went wrong, we could end up in bankruptcy, but it seemed the solution was there on my desk, staring me in the face.

For the first time in our cautious lives, we decided to take a leap of faith. Susie and I resolved that we were going to live in that house. We accepted several new credit cards, the weather broke, and we resumed work.

That's when the miracles started to happen. We disliked wallboard and wanted expensive knotty-pine interior walls. I drove to the lumber company, and there was a truckload of knotty-pine boards sitting in the parking lot with a sign that said $108, a tiny fraction of its value. I told them to deliver it.

For the ceilings I didn't mind wallboard so much, but I realized I couldn't put the heavy sheets up by myself. This time there was a truckload of pine shiplap boards in the lumber company parking lot for the same ridiculous price.

We wanted high quality lighting and settled on some schoolhouse style fixtures that were expensive. We needed five but held off on buying them because our credit line was dwindling fast. By then, my unemployment had run out, and I had taken a part-time job in a furniture store. One day my boss came in with a box of five schoolhouse light fixtures that he had bought years before. I hadn't told him I was looking for light fixtures, let alone this particular style. He just thought I could use them.

We wanted wood panel doors, not the less expensive hollow type. The father of one of our daughter's playmates offered us serviceable panel doors that he had salvaged from a junkyard.

That spring we needed at least eight loads of topsoil to cover the septic system. I noticed that some men were deepening the ditches on our road, and I asked them if they wanted a place to dump the rich silt they were digging out. They dumped twenty loads on our property, enough to do the whole yard.

And so it went. On the Fourth of July, one year after we had started the framing, we moved in and started putting our rent toward our credit card payments. The house was in rough shape: no flooring, no siding, few windows. But it was livable—and it was ours.

It took another two years of part-time work to finish it. By the time it was finished, I had decided to attend graduate school in the Midwest. Building the house had expanded my vision enough that I could actually contemplate doing something more fulfilling with my life. Just days after pounding in the last nail, we sold our dream house and moved out. The money paid off the credit cards and bought us a house near my new university.

People ask if we've ever regretted giving up the dream house we worked on so hard. The answer is no—the house was our teacher. It taught us that we can do what we want with our lives despite seemingly insurmountable obstacles. To this day, we keep a picture of the house on our dresser. It is a constant reminder of what we can do when we set our minds to it.

Michael Murphy

Pause and Reflect

1. Are you stuck in old familiar routines? What holds you back from taking a leap into the unknown?
2. When was the last time you decided to do something differently? What was the outcome? Examine your resistance to doing things differently from time to time.

Life Lesson #6:
Think Global

Whether I like it or not, I am on this planet and it is far better to do something for humanity.

THE 14TH DALAI LAMA OF TIBET

There's an old saying, "It's a small world." And we've probably all had the experience of running into people we know in faraway places where we never would have expected to see them. The world is indeed smaller than we sometimes imagine. In the 1960s, social psychologist Stanley Milgram formulated the small-world method, which inspired the concept "six degrees of separation." The idea is that anyone in the world can connect with anyone else in the world in a mere six steps. You start by contacting someone you know, who then contacts someone he or she knows, and so on. Six billion people . . . and every one of them only six steps away from you, whether "The president of the United States, a gondolier in Venice, just fill in the names . . . " says a character in John Guare's play *Six Degrees of Separation.*

Perhaps now, in the twenty-first century, there are even fewer than six steps between us all. With the Internet, it's easy to announce our presence and allow the world to beat a path to our door. And as we make all these connections with others near and far, it becomes clear that our diverse world—political disputes and wars notwithstanding—is becoming one interconnected global system. It is as if we are all individual neurons in an awakening global brain. What we think and do affects others on a global scale as never before. Like it or not, the role of "global citizen" is being thrust upon us.

How will we rise to the challenges of global citizenry? First, we must realize that *the world is my family.* Media coverage ensures that we no longer isolate ourselves from the harsh realities of the world—natural disasters, malnourished children, mothers dying of AIDS, fathers trying to find food for their families, war-torn cities where people live their lives never knowing where or when the next bomb will go off. Sometimes peace feels futile, and the abolishment of hunger and poverty from Earth hopeless visions that should have happened a long time ago. Sometimes we wonder how we could ever make a difference in the face of these things.

But you don't have to travel to other countries or work for an international organization to be a global citizen or make a difference on a global level. Start local. Start in your own house. Annual Earth Day activities now bring attention to a myriad of things we can do in our immediate home and office environments to contribute to a lessening of global warming and the greening of our planet. *American*

Idol raised $30 million for charities in Africa and the United States, introducing a whole new generation of young people to the joy of philanthropy.

And the work of Japanese scientist Dr. Masaru Emoto has shown that even our thoughts influence the world around us. Dr. Emoto has photographed the crystal structures of water samples taken before and after prayer; before and after exposure to various kinds of music, such as heavy metal and Beethoven; and to words with very different intentions, such as "You make me sick; I will kill you," versus "Love and appreciation." The energies from beautiful words and thoughts, even if only written, create exquisite snowflake-like patterns in the water crystals. The less uplifting energies create images of disorder and toxicity. From Dr. Emoto's work we have learned that the simple act of just saying "thank you" can influence the world in a positive way.

We are bigger than we think. Our influence spreads wider than we know. "One thought fills immensity," wrote the poet William Blake.

And in the words written by Ted Perry for a 1971 environmental movie (commonly attributed to Chief Seattle): "This we know: the Earth does not belong to man, man belongs to the Earth. All things are connected like the blood that unites us all."

The following story is about one man who understands this connection—and lives it every day of his life.

☕ The Global Citizen: A Love Story

I grew up in a small Oklahoma town. I was raised in a happy, religious home, had perfect attendance in Sunday school, and was an A student. But I often felt that I didn't fully belong where I was. I was taught to "love thy neighbor," but noticed that the African Americans who worked in our town actually lived outside it in other small towns, to which they returned every day after work.

This subtle awareness of social issues was furthered by a small current events newspaper we got in elementary school. Even at that young age, I was touched to read about the United Nations. I sensed something beautiful and expansive about an organization concerned with the whole Earth and the understanding that everyone should have an adequate life.

By the time I reached college, I strongly disliked social injustice of any kind. I became active in the civil rights and women's rights movements—and even led a protest over a policy prohibiting female students from wearing pants in the library and having a curfew! But my first great awakening occurred when, in my junior year, a group of fellow students and I drove to Chicago for a weekend seminar on the Theological Revolution of the 20th Century, conducted by the Ecumenical Institute.

The seminar was held in an African-American ghetto, where the institute was trying to create a model of renewed community. The contrasts were great: I was used to neat Oklahoma towns and a well-kept college campus; here I was surrounded by broken glass, burned-out cars, and garbage.

But something even more astonishing was happening inside, at the seminar. We were dialoguing with some of the greatest theologians of our time, discussing age-old questions about divinity, the reality of life, and the search for meaning. By the end of the weekend, I was experiencing the truth of Paul Tillich's teaching, that each of us is fully "accepted" just as we are. We don't have to seek another life, another situation, or another condition; our life is perfect just as it is. Before the weekend, I had often felt shy and alienated; I now felt an interior explosion of healing and goodness and perfection.

And I wanted to share that! After a month-long course at the institute in the ghetto right after graduating, I realized I had a mission—I *was* a mission. I could give my life to helping create a different kind of world, where everyone could realize their potential. I attended theological seminary and decided to intern with the institute. I fell in love with a wonderful woman and we married. But I would also soon fall in love with and marry a beautiful planet. It was to be my second great awakening.

By this time the Ecumenical Institute had evolved into its secular form, the Institute of Cultural Affairs. This institute was all about helping people realize what was possible, and creating a new world of justice, peace, and hope. A group of institute colleagues decided to take a trip around the world, not as tourists, but as people who wanted to know, *How can we open ourselves to the raw experience of the world—to its beauty, its suffering, its reality, its diversity?* We wanted passionately to be in intimate dialogue with it all.

Our plan was ambitious: around the world in thirty-two days. By changing cultures every two or three days—customs, climate, terrain, food, language—we knew we would create a sensory, psychological, mythic, and spiritual overload. And that's what we wanted: not just to observe the world, but to be the world—the world we wanted to serve.

As we touched down around the globe, I was filled with awe by our planet's vast oceans, jagged peaks, sprawling cities, wildly diverse cultures, and masses of beautiful people. I experienced the powerful mystery of the Aztecs; the sublime beauty of a Shinto shrine; the vitality of Hong Kong; the sultry weather of Manila; the serenity of the

Emerald Buddha; a live-goat sacrifice in a Hindu temple; a visit with the China Lama in Kathmandu; the site where Buddha had his enlightenment and gave his first sermon; the devastating poverty of Calcutta; the birthday celebration of Emperor Haile Selassie in Addis Ababa; the decaying grandeur of Greek and Roman civilization; the awesome beauty of the Vatican; the wonders of a medieval walled city in Dubrovnik; a coming-home experience in the British Isles; and the eternal day of Iceland.

Our accommodations were simple: a church basement, a small hotel. Conditions were often uncomfortable. My little hotel room in New Delhi felt like a blast furnace from the hot wind blowing through. Sometimes we were sick. I became dizzy and almost fainted when I saw that goat killed in Nepal. But we wanted to experience what other people experience.

At the end of the adventure, we stopped in Iceland, where all twenty-five of us shared our thoughts about everything we had encountered, trying to "squeeze the meaning" out of our experience. We had become global citizens. We had discovered that while cultures may be different, people are the same. Everyone wants enough food and shelter. They want to be happy and they want their children to be happy. They have different symbols; they might eat with chopsticks or a fork; they might have a statue or an image or no image. But the human striving is first to survive, then go beyond survival to beauty and truth and union with the divine.

After that trip, I was never, ever the same. I was in love with the Earth and with humanity at large. I had been touched by tragic suffering, sublime beauty, spiritual genius, by the ecstasy of being human on this magnificent planet. I had come home. I had been hugged by Mother Earth—and I had to respond. I had to give my life, my love, my action—to make a difference, to relieve suffering, to advance the human condition. Nothing else would be enough. As a child of the Earth, a child of Humanity, I knew it was my duty to serve my people and my planet.

Before this time I had never left my own nation. After this time I would spend thirty-five years living, working, and visiting in fifty-five countries around the world.

For the next twenty years, with my wife and two young sons, I lived and worked in urban slums and poor rural villages in Malaysia, the Republic of Korea, the United States, Jamaica, and Venezuela. We were not well-paid consultants driving in to give advice to the poor. In a Korean village we lived in a rock and mud thatched-roof house. In Jamaica our sons attended a one-room school house with 300 students in a mountain village. I was passionately committed to changing human history, to helping reinvent societies that worked for everyone.

But my childhood reveries came true when I was asked

to work for the United Nations. My UN passport was a tangible, magical symbol of my global citizenship. I was being called to transpose my experience from the grassroots project level to the global policy level.

I have helped local peoples around the world improve sanitation, waste management, recycling, water supplies, air quality, environmental health, education, and income. I have helped them prevent depletion of shellfish stocks in Brazil, plant trees in Egypt, and dig drainage ditches in Tanzania. I have been overwhelmed with the vitality, hope, and hard work of local people regardless of nation, culture, or religion, whether rural or urban, women or men. The heroes were always the local people. I was only a catalyst, a choreographer of change, a social artist.

This small-town Oklahoma boy has lived his life in love with the world; and what a beautiful world it is—full of suffering and happiness, squalor and grandeur. I have received infinitely more gifts from my beloved than I have given her. She is much more gracious and generous, lavishing joy and sorrow, understanding and mystery, with immense and exquisite compassion.

And how does my love story with the Earth continue? My wife of thirty-five years has passed on and my sons are grown men. I am ready for the next global/local adventure! In fact, having recently retired from the UN, I am on a one-year sabbatical that includes becoming engaged to a most amazing woman, consulting for the UN, teaching graduate school to international students, caring for my elderly mother, and developing my dancing skills. What will life offer and require of me, and you, next? Whatever it is, "We are the people and now is the time!"

Moorman Robertson Work Jr.

Pause and Reflect

Make a list of four ways in which you can act as a global rather than a local citizen—even by doing something at home. Some examples might be to get off the mailing lists of catalogs you're not using, or buying energy-saving light bulbs for your home.

Essential Ingredient #2

FILLING YOUR OWN CUP

The most enlightened prayer isn't "Dear
God, send me someone wonderful," but,
"Dear God, help me realize that
I am someone wonderful."

Marianne Williamson

LIFE LESSON #1:
LOVE YOUR BODY, LOVE YOURSELF

*Enjoy your body. Use it every way you can. Don't
be afraid of it or of what other people think of it.
It's the greatest instrument you'll ever own.*

KURT VONNEGUT

I sat in my therapist's office, crying. "It doesn't matter how much I do—it's never enough!" I shouted angrily. "I take my supplements, I do yoga every day, I come regularly for my appointments. I still can't balance my pH, and my cancer still won't go away."

Ali, my therapist, sat in compassionate silence while I sobbed. Then, quietly, he said, "I think the problem, Jennifer, is that you make healing an item on your to-do list. You think it's something you can 'do'—like going to the grocery store or picking up the dry cleaning—then check off your list when you've completed it. But you're not willing to change anything about your routine, your habits, your workaholism, your thriving on adrenaline. You don't make taking care of yourself a priority, and you're not willing to live your life any differently." I left his office in despair, knowing he was right.

Three years earlier, a doctor had discovered I had a basal cell carcinoma on the side of my nose. Chemotherapy had cured it—for one year. When it came back, I knew I had to do more.

So I had determined to change my diet and work with Ali, a psychologist and health practitioner, to see if I could eliminate the cause of the disease. At this point I had been trying for a year and a half, but the cancer was visibly growing. In complete frustration, I finally scheduled an appointment to see a doctor for a biopsy. I felt that I had failed.

I was relieved to be going on vacation to Hawaii before the appointment. I desperately needed a break, having worked twelve to fourteen hours a day in the final days before to meet a work deadline. I was exhausted—physically, mentally, and emotionally. I knew that what Ali was saying was true, but I didn't have a clue how to change my life. To make matters worse, my frenetic pace had been completely at odds with what I was writing and speaking about—topics like balance! But I couldn't see how to do things differently and still meet my deadlines. Not meeting deadlines and speaking demands would have been unthinkable for me.

Once in Hawaii, I did almost nothing but rest. I walked on the beach at beautiful Lanikai on Oahu, then slept, then walked some more. I had little energy for anything else, and I cried every day. I prayed for answers and met frequently with friends in a support circle.

One day I met Ginny. Before I met her, I thought I knew how to take care of myself—despite what Ali had said to me.

I thought I knew what self-love was. I had been speaking professionally about self-esteem for more than ten years, always defining it as how much you like yourself. But as many times as I had stood in front of audiences and talked about how self-esteem is deeper than achievements, deeper than possessions, deeper than relationships—I was defining my own self-worth by exactly that: my material and outward success.

What was missing for me was the understanding that in order to heal the body you actually need to have a relationship with it. You cannot put your healing on your to-do list. You have to get very real, willing to go deep within yourself, to expose yourself, to become vulnerable *to yourself,* and to show yourself that you care.

This will mean different things to different people. But I've shared Ginny's story with you because perhaps, like me, you will read it and come away with a deeper understanding of what self-love means—and how it demands a new relationship with our bodies. If not making friends with our bodies, we've at least got to open a dialog.

As for me, Ginny helped me understand that self-love is really compassion directed towards one's self. Her story went so deep into my mind and heart that I did begin talking to my body, appreciating it in a new way. And one month after meeting Ginny, I canceled my doctor's appointment. My cancer was gone.

It was ten o'clock at night and all was silent on the hospital ward. I went to the bathroom to wash and looked into the mirror. I saw my bald head, the dark circles under my eyes, and my skinny body wounded from six months of cancer treatment.

The irony of my situation was not lost on me. As a child I was an avid swimmer, and at seventeen, I qualified for the 1964 Olympics 100-meter freestyle event. Although my Olympic dream was never realized, I continued to swim and then coach swimming. For the next thirty years I stayed in peak condition and broke five national Masters Swimming records for my age group!

Meanwhile, my professional life was flourishing. I had moved west to Santa Fe, New Mexico, to pursue my calling as an artist. Now, at the age of fifty, I was a regionally known sculptor and loved my work—carving stone and creating bronzes.

Then, in August 1997, I was diagnosed with advanced breast cancer. The doctors told me the cancer had probably been growing for eight to ten years, and during surgery, a tumor the size of an orange was removed. For the next nine months I embraced conventional treatment with the attitude that I would pull out all the stops and take a stand for my life. I embraced acupuncture, meditation, even a macrobiotic diet—and sailed through three months of chemotherapy with no ill effects. At one point I asked Lama Dorje, a Tibetan monk in Santa Fe, about cancer. He said, "Ginny, do not be fearful. Fear increases illness. Do whatever medicine you choose; it does not matter. Be joyful! Do what makes you happy!" And I felt happy, despite cancer.

Finally, my doctor recommended a risky new treatment called "stem cell rescue," in which stem cells are extracted from bone marrow, frozen, and later put back into the body after high doses of chemotherapy have theoretically destroyed all cancer cells.

The treatment, which I took as an outpatient, was brutal. I threw up, fainted, had epileptic seizures, and suffered internal bleeding, as well as a nosebleed that lasted seven hours—my platelets were so low that my blood couldn't clot. I lost fifteen pounds and was skin and bones. After the stem cells were reintroduced, I was just waiting for the tenth day, when the stem cells should have kicked in and start rebuilding my immune system. But on day nine my white blood cell count was below fifty so I had to be admitted to the hospital. My doctor said my immune system was so depleted that if I scratched myself, I could infect myself and die.

In my hospital room there was a large notice on the door stating "Neutropoenic"—which, loosely translated, meant that I could die if someone breathed on me. The nurses and doctors said it would be up to two months before my immune system returned to normal—if it ever did. I could not have visitors and would be alone a lot.

Now here I was, late at night, regarding myself in the mirror, as bald as Tweety Bird. I looked like Death.

And then something odd happened. Friends had always told me, "Ginny, you need to love yourself." Never having experienced unconditional love, I had no idea what it felt like. But in that moment, looking in the mirror at my wounded body, a deep feeling came up from my belly, and I started to cry.

For the first time, I felt compassion for me. Tears came down my cheeks as I gently bathed my body the way a mother would bathe an infant. I pressed the hot washcloth against my skin with love and compassion, saying "I love you" and "thank you" with every touch. For the first time, I felt unconditional love for myself.

That night I went to sleep feeling safe and happy. I knew I would live through this, and I made a promise to help others heal from cancer if I did.

When I woke up it was sunrise over the Sandia Mountains. I felt so good that I danced around the room singing my favorite song, Bobby McFerrin's "Don't Worry, Be Happy."

The nurse took my blood sample. Minutes later, the doctor returned with my report. Suddenly, he shouted *"What?"*

The nurses came running; they probably thought I had died! He said, "Yesterday her blood counts were 600. Today they are 7,700. They're normal!"

He said the only reason they would be so high was if I had a fever or an infection, but I had neither. And I had been there only three days! The nurses said they had not seen anyone recover so quickly. The next day they sent me home.

Less than two weeks later, I heard about a Chinese exercise called Chi-Lel, the form of medical qigong (pronounced "chee-gung"), considered the number-one self-healing method for chronic illness in China. Watching a videotape, I gazed in awe as an ultrasound showed a patient's bladder tumor disappear in forty-five seconds while four teachers said affirmations and waved their hands over the area of the tumor, never even touching his body!

Thrilled by this discovery, I went to a workshop to learn Chi-Lel for myself—and found that one of the techniques involved patting the body with the center of the palms while "talking" to the body. It was almost identical to what I had done spontaneously that night in the hospital.

At the workshop, my teacher suggested I begin teaching others, and over the next four months I taught 800 people. Healings occurred regularly; I had been shown a way to help others, as well as myself.

In the following years, practicing Chi-Lel would help me complete my physical, emotional, and mental healing, as well as detoxify my body from the conventional treatments I had received. My oncologist said that the cancer would probably be back within a year, but I have now been cancer free for eight years. I call my new hair my $100,000 haircut! In 2002 I was promoted to senior instructor of Chi-Lel, one of only five worldwide, and I have now taught this self-healing method to more than three thousand people.

Most important is the emotional healing I've experienced. My heart has opened and I feel like everyone is my family. When I learned how to feel compassion for myself, I learned how to feel compassion for everyone. Compassion has allowed me to feel a oneness with all of life—and this has empowered me as a woman, an artist, and a human being.

Virginia Whiting Walden

Pause and Reflect

1. When you look in the mirror, what do you say to yourself? Find three things about your body that you like.
2. See if you can go one day without making a single negative comment about your body to yourself or to another.
3. When do you feel the most "beautiful"?

LIFE LESSON #2:
LEARN THE LANGUAGE OF YOUR BODY

You need to listen to your body, because your
body is listening to you.

PHILIP C. McGRAW, AKA DR. PHIL

The movement toward alternative medicine, health, and exercise is catching on like wildfire in this country. Yoga has gone mainstream, and universities are establishing colleges of alternative healing. "Integrative medicine" is an emerging field of Western medicine that seeks to meld the best of complementary and alternative therapies with the best of mainstream medicine. And "wholeness," a word that describes mind/body/spirit fitness and integration, is no longer the sole property of New Age thinking.

As Deepak Chopra, a pioneer in the field of mind/body medicine, says in his book *Unconditional Life*, "Medical science was not being true to reality until it conceded that illness is connected to a person's emotions, beliefs, and expectations."[1]

I am well aware of the miracles of Western medicine, including the surgeries I have had that have made my life better. My mother's life has been saved on more than one occasion by the quick thinking and acting of medical professionals. My gratitude is deep and eternal.

But intuitively I feel that we must take a deeper look at what is happening on a collective level when it comes to healing. I am appalled at the take-a-pill mentality we see in every other commercial during primetime television— all ending with the disclaimer about the possible side effects of the drug (a natural outcome of the symptoms-based approach).

I'd like to see us start taking care of ourselves in a way that removes the need to take most prescription drugs.

I'd also like to see us start looking beyond the physical for answers to physical symptoms. We can start by listening to our bodies.

Mackey McNeill's story is an almost unbelievable tale of how a deep emotional wound manifested itself as a frightening physical symptom—and how it was healed. It is a story that reminds us that true healing can only take place from the perspective of wholeness, based on the remembrance that everything is connected.

Blurry Vision

As a CPA and financial planner, I usually had a practical view of life. But a few years ago a medical concern radically altered this approach.

It all started one morning as I was driving to my office.

Suddenly, for a few seconds, the road looked blurry. The fuzzy vision continued on and off for the entire journey. I became frantic, imagining I had some horrible disease.

Over the next few weeks, I bounced from doctor to doctor, first an ophthalmologist, followed by a GP, neurologist, and an ear, nose, and throat specialist. No one could find anything wrong. I continued to experience random moments of blurry vision.

Sitting in church one day, the problem recurred. I closed one eye. To my surprise, I could see perfectly; the problem was only in my left eye! I returned to the neurologist, who diagnosed a twitch in the muscles surrounding my left eye. He offered me a prescription to take "daily and forever."

I went home in despair. I was tired of being poked and prodded, and viewed in terms of "pieces." A pill was not a cure. My goal was a permanent healing, but I had no idea what to do next. I flopped down in my favorite chair and picked up a magazine I liked—and just happened to turn to an article on "energy healers."

I was intrigued by the suggestion that physical symptoms often relate to previous life events where we shut down and bypassed our feelings. The article suggested these "bypass" moments set up energetic blocks in our body. Remove the block, cure the symptom. That sounded like the solution I was seeking.

I've always been willing to try anything once—but

where in the world would I find an energy healer? Two days later, in perfect synchronicity, a friend recommended one. I immediately made an appointment. Arriving at the healer's house, I felt nervous. The article said energy healers were intuitive, and I wondered if she would be able to read my mind. The whole thing felt strange.

She escorted me to her simple workroom. As I lay on the massage table, she held her hands over my body. "I'm feeling your energy," she explained. Her quiet confidence was reassuring, and I felt my doubts melting away.

Although I had not disclosed my problem, she said she felt an energy block over my left eye. I was amazed! She asked me if I had injured my eye. Startled, I remembered that four years before, I had lost my balance playing racquetball and hit my head, producing an egg-sized knot and a black left eye.

She asked me to tell her more about the events surrounding this injury. I explained that I had been adopted as an infant. A few weeks before the accident, I had met my birth family for the first time. I'd planned to visit them again the day after my accident, but I canceled my trip because of my injuries.

She continued her work. I relaxed and fell asleep.

In the week that followed, only one incident of blurred vision occurred. I arrived for my next appointment feeling optimistic. She asked about my relationship with my birth parents. I said they were loving people who had welcomed me graciously back into their family. While our reunion had been joyful, I was challenged to deal with two sets of parents. In a month, my birth parents were taking the entire family on a cruise.

"How do you feel about that?"

"Grateful."

"And what else?"

I did not want to admit to any other feelings.

"Do you want to heal your eye?" she asked.

"Well, there are these little nagging thoughts," I said. As tears flowed, the thoughts and feelings tumbled out. "My birth parents have enough money to treat us to a cruise. Yet when I was born, they thought there wasn't enough money to keep me. I would rather have stayed with them than go on this cruise now. I missed thirty-eight years with them and my heart aches!"

As I expressed my buried feelings, I felt guilty, as if I were betraying my adoptive parents, who had given me unconditional love. My feelings also seemed like a slap in the face to my birth parents. Yet I could no longer deny my deep sorrow and anger.

"Repress your feelings and you will rob yourself of your healing," the healer said. "Feelings are neither right nor wrong. They just are. Accept and release them. Here are your options. Tell your birth parents how you feel, and get well. Say nothing, go on the cruise, and get deathly ill. You choose!"

I thought, *How can I tell these kind people I'm angry?*

Then my real fear surfaced: *If I express my resentment, they might reject me!*

Four days later, I called my birth parents. I was in tears before I could speak. "I need to talk to you. My intention is that love be present at the end of this call." I took a few deep breaths to ease the pain in my chest. Then one of the most magical moments of my life occurred. My birth parents said, "You can say anything to us, and we will love you. We have always loved you and always will."

Skeptical of receiving love, between sobs I said, "You may change your mind. I'm grateful for the gift, but I'm angry. The years I missed feel like a deep hole in my heart." Now we were all crying.

My birth parents told me again, "We have always loved you and always will."

The pain in my chest began to lessen. Rejection, my worst fear, had not come to pass. I was filled with joy and peace.

After this conversation, I never again had blurry vision. The cruise was fabulous as I grew closer to my birth family. Filled with happiness, I could hardly stay in my skin as I celebrated my birthday surrounded by my birth family for the first time.

My healing enabled me to see that the physical and the emotional are not separate. My experience taught me to trust my physical body as a gateway to my intuition. My body speaks with clarity—and it never lies. Now I pay attention to my aches and tight spots, recognizing them as messengers, alerting me to discover what else might be present.

Developing intuition is like learning any new skill: it feels awkward at first, but if you persevere, it becomes as natural as breathing. Today I live a wildly prosperous life, built by listening, following, and acting upon my own inner wisdom.

For me, this is what it truly means to heal.

Mackey McNeill

Pause and Reflect

1. What or who inspires you, and why? Are you living according to what most inspires you? What was your childhood dream and what happened to it? What changes would you have to make to ensure that what inspires you becomes more of a practical guiding principle in your life?
2. Pay attention this week to the things that claim your interest. Notice if any of these things draw your attention because they inspire you.

LIFE LESSON #3:
LET YOUR BODY MOVE YOU

I measure time by how the body sways.

THEODORE ROETHKE

One of the fastest ways I've found to get out of misery is to put on some music and move! As Gabrielle Roth, creator of "The Five Rhythms," says, "Put the psyche in motion, and it will heal itself."[1] I have discovered that even five minutes of dancing to music I love can shift my mood, release stuck emotions, energize me, and make me a nicer person.

But there are all kinds of ways to move our bodies, and one of the best and easiest is walking. The woman affectionately known in my neighborhood as "the dog lady" walks by my house every day. She is one of those people who bear an uncanny likeness to their pets: she is sleek, silver-haired, and eager. She is also devoted, because no matter how beautiful or brutal our weather, she's out there twice a day with her two greyhounds, who think they're walking her.

"Why?" I asked her one day.

"It gives me purpose and timing," she said. "Like the lines on a calendar, it shows me where I am now, in my day, and in my life."

Elinor is another walker. About five times a week she heads for Snow Canyon, just minutes from her house, and spends some time communing with rocks. They speak to her. Although she's been a regular walker for fifteen years, she says this walk is like a walking meditation: it's a time just to be. She doesn't listen to headphones, doesn't focus on anything, doesn't try to solve problems, but enjoys nature and connects to the earth. If something has been "up," the answer usually comes to her on the way out of the park, at the edge, in what she calls her "ah-hah" zone.

And then there's my friend Jennifer. Walking in Central Park every single morning of her life is her lifeline. Like Ashley (the dog lady), Jennifer doesn't really care how bad the latest ice storm blanketing the Northeast is. Never mind that she walks all over New York the rest of the day, putting in miles between subway stops, grocery stores, the florist, and the restaurant where she eats at 11:00 PM on her way home. She says there's a tree there that moves her to tears.

We've long heard about the benefits of walking: more energy, deeper and more satisfying sleep, stronger leg muscles. Walkers are said to live longer and have less incidence of cancer, heart disease, stroke, diabetes, and other "killer" diseases. It impacts mind and spirit, too. One website says it "benefits your brain power, improves your mood and helps ward off depression, and allows you to connect more deeply with your spiritual side and with your loved ones."[2]

I've heard Dr. Deepak Chopra say many times that walking is the ultimate exercise because every part of the body is affected. And it can work quickly, giving you fast results in the way you look and feel.

So the next story, by Staci Richmond, does not surprise—but it does inspire. You read it while I go for a walk.

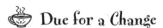 Due for a Change

One of the harshest realities I have ever faced was when my youngest son was well into toddlerhood, and I still looked like I was in my second trimester of pregnancy. I had four children ranging from two to eight years of age. I had put career plans on hold and had been a stay-at-home mom for six years. Somewhere between the comings and goings of my husband's and children's lives, I had made mine.

"Me time" was not just hard to come by, it was nonexistent. Like a lot of moms, I erroneously believed that putting myself on the back burner and putting the needs of my family first made me a better mother. I couldn't work out; I was too busy driving the car pool. I couldn't do Tae-bo; I was exhausted from chasing the kids. When the children napped, I crashed, too. And I certainly couldn't get my nails done or go to a day spa; we were a one-income family of six.

Late at night, when the kids were finally asleep and the dishes done, I would soak my exhausted carcass in a bubble bath and dream of the future, when I could get my nails done, when I would have time to be Denise Austin.

What I learned—albeit the hard way—was that when it comes to making time for myself, there is no time like the present.

The truth snuck up on me one sunny April morning. I was in-between library story time and a play date when my gurgling stomach reminded me I had forgotten to eat breakfast. I stopped for a doughnut at the gas station, and as I waited to pay, the young woman behind the counter looked at me, smiled sweetly, and asked, "When are you due?"

Due for what? An oil change? I've got another 1,000 miles to go, thanks.

"How much longer until you have your baby?" she inquired again. I was going to let the first question go, but this girl was determined to shatter my self-esteem.

"I am not pregnant," I said, through clenched teeth.

"Oh. So you just had the baby!" she bubbled.

"Two years ago," I screeched, my ears turning red.

"Oh," she giggled. "I guess I had you confused with

another short-haired lady who comes in here."

Another overweight, short-haired lady, I thought, scowling.

The most violent thoughts I've ever had in my life did the tango in my mind. The truth not only hurt, it haunted me.

I crawled from that station, a two-ton Tessie, brewing and stewing.

I'm not that fat, I told myself, looking into a full-length mirror.

"Do you think Mommy is fat?" I asked my children at dinner.

"No, Mom," my oldest daughter said. "You're huggable."

"You look okay in clothes," my son chimed in, adding, "but you shouldn't go anywhere naked."

While I admired his honesty, his assessment did nothing to help me sleep that night. Gas-station girl's wounding words had resonated with me. Tossing and turning, I vowed to wage a personal war against fat.

The next morning, I dragged myself out of bed and readied myself for a walk. I put on my sweats and tennis shoes and looked in the mirror again. Either I'd lost weight overnight or I wasn't coherent enough for my eyes to focus properly, but I liked what I saw.

"Lookin' good," I mused, giving myself a little wink as I strutted toward the door.

I let determination set my pace, swinging my arms. I built momentum, reaching the end of the first block in record time. I passed my neighbor but was too winded to exchange pleasantries. I persisted, and when a jogger sprinted by with perfect form, I thought confidently, *I could take her.*

I was on the final stretch of the three-mile course I'd set for myself. Somewhere in the distance, I thought I heard the theme song from *Rocky* playing.

"I think I can, I think I can," I chugged.

Coming down the home stretch, I kicked it into high gear. I lapped the paper boy. Perspiration ran down my face and splashed onto the sidewalk. No one could catch me. The insults of a thousand, thoughtless thugs would not deter me.

"I am woman, hear me roar," I wailed, rounding the bend.

I made it home, exhausted, sweaty, and fired up for the day, the attack on my dignity from the day before driving my success. *Eat your heart out, gas-station girl,* I thought. I came, I conquered, and I didn't even stop for a doughnut!

That walk was the first of many. I lost almost 80 pounds walking, and although over the past several years admittedly my weight has fluctuated, I have been at my very best physically, mentally, and emotionally when I've been walking regularly. My kids notice it, too. If I get a little agitated or become short-tempered, my daughter will say, "Why don't you go for a walk?"

I am someone who has difficulty saying no to others. A martyr at heart, I will say yes without blinking to cooking dinner for fifty people at my church. I will say yes to serving on another committee—even if I'm already on twelve. Just as I did when my children were little, there are times even now when I drive myself to the point of physical and mental fatigue giving to others. I have had to learn—and now and again I need a reminder—that it is not necessarily selfish to say no to the charity benefit and yes to a massage. The bottom line is, if a person isn't good to herself, she can't be good to anybody else. In that light, taking time for a pedicure or a trip to the gym isn't an act of selfishness, it's an act of altruism.

My ten-year-old son confirmed this just the other day. I bought a new outfit, the first I'd bought in a long time. My friend Roger said to the kids, "It's great that your mom did something nice for herself for a change."

My son beamed, "Well, it wasn't just for *her,* it was for us, too. When our mom looks good, that makes us look good. When she feels good, we all feel good."

I couldn't have said it better myself.

Staci Ann Richmond

Pause and Reflect

1. What kind of exercise, if any, are you currently doing, and is it something you love to do, or something you think you "should" be doing?
2. Keep a daily journal that tracks how you feel before and after exercise. Is there a correlation between low spirits and low exercise? Take the time to ask yourself whether enjoying the exercise makes a difference in how you feel afterward.

Life Lesson #4:
Make the Mind/Body/Spirit Connection

Better keep yourself clean and bright; you are the
window through which you must see the world.

George Bernard Shaw

Being in nature, walking, making love, and exercising are all ways to help us get grounded, centered, connected, and feeling good in our bodies. Applying our creativity to working on a project or reading a good book can feed our minds. All of these things can nurture our spirits, too. The important thing is that *all three* must be nourished if balance and serenity are what we're looking for.

But if we think we're doing everything possible to nurture our minds, bodies, and spirits, we may be deluding ourselves if we have not addressed the ways in which we "medicate" ourselves in order not to feel.

Alcohol and drugs are the obvious medicators, but also common in our culture are addictions to caffeine, sugar, food, gambling, sex, television, sun-worshipping, relationships, work, worry—anything or any process over which we have no control. It's significant that one out of four people in our culture suffers from addiction.[1]

I never thought of myself as an addict, because I don't use chemical substances and rarely drink a glass of wine.

Without realizing it, however, I struggled with the one addiction ironically lauded and encouraged by our society: workaholism. We think that an employee willing to consistently work overtime is a gift! But we could not be more wrong.

Workaholism usually involves an addiction to adrenaline, a self-generated chemical. I have known many days when I was *unable* to stop working because the adrenaline was pumping so fast. I wouldn't take time, even on weekends, to be with my family. I wouldn't take a break to go outside on a beautiful day to enjoy some sunshine and fresh air. Sometimes it was hard for me even to stop for a bathroom break.

To make matters worse, all these behaviors occurred as I was working on a book—about balance! All the signals were there telling me I was off track. But none was as loud as the one coming from my body. It was screaming. My back hurt all the time from hunching over a computer. My eyes were blurry and strained by the end of the day (or night). My neck was in constant need of adjustment. The only way I could relax was to get into a hot bath.

So I believe it when addiction experts like Anne Wilson Schaef say that, like any disease, addiction is progressive and will lead to death unless we actively recover from it. I have had to look hard at my disease and how it affects my family life, my health, and my happiness. It has created so much pain for me, stopping me from experiencing intimacy with my loved ones, that even writing about it makes me cry.

I am "in recovery" for my work addiction, but constantly challenged by the temptation to overschedule my activities and push beyond the level of my body's comfort and ease. I continue to get help in my efforts to heal it.

But I am definitely trying. As my friend Rosie says, "If you don't take care of your body, where will you live?"

So I practice yoga several times a week. I walk whenever I can. But most of all, I don't let adrenaline run me any more. Instead of working long hours at my computer, I take breaks to lie across my Swiss ball and allow my chest area to open. I'll take time to get laundry going or wash dishes (a real plus of having a home office). I'll call a friend to catch up, even if it's just for a few minutes. I'm open to meeting friends for lunch outside my home, rather than eating in my office. And with only rare exceptions, I leave my evenings open for connecting with those I care about, watching a movie, or reading the latest book that's caught my attention.

I've also learned that anything that demands being done in a hurry is probably not worth doing. Putting pressure on myself is definitely not good for my body, soul, or mental health.

Chellie Campbell's story is an example of recognizing that she, too, was in trouble and needed help. Chellie says that eliminating addictive chemicals is just as much a spiritual undertaking as a physical one. And it's the mental decision that enables both healings to take place. Her inspiring story reminds us that mind, body, and spirit cannot be separated, so it doesn't really matter where you start. Just start.

My Name Is Chellie C.

My name is Chellie C., and I'm an alcoholic. This is my story of what it was like, what happened, and what it is like now. Some of you will recognize this beginning as the standard opening for a speaker at an Alcoholics Anonymous meeting. Others may not know it, but will come to know it in the future. I, too, was once blithely unaware of my deepening dependence on alcohol.

It started as a simple habit—just a glass of wine when I got home from work. It "took the edge off" a hard day's work and helped me relax. Insidiously, when the hard day became a little harder, the glass of wine became two. Then, in classic alcoholic denial, I bought *bigger* glasses so I could still say I only had two glasses of wine. I wonder whom I thought I was fooling.

I had my reasons for drinking. I was under a lot of stress. I was teaching financial stress reduction workshops and I was the most financially stressed person in the room. I was trying to keep my small business alive after having lost a $300,000-a-year account. I was trying to pay off the $80,000 credit card debt; trying to sell the $160,000 condo that was now worth only $90,000; trying to forget the deaths of my mother, my uncle, my aunt, my cousin's baby, my best friend. I was trying to keep up appearances as a business owner, president of a business group, and board member of my Rotary Club. I put my game face on every day and washed it off with alcohol every night.

Of course, I knew I had a problem. I even knew I had to do something about it. I knew about Alcoholics Anonymous and "one day at a time." Every morning, I'd say, "Just for today I won't have a drink." And I'd keep that promise until I got home from work. And then I would have a drink. Finally, I had to face the fact that I could not go one day without a drink. Not one day.

Finally, I hit bottom. My liquor cabinet was bare and I went to the grocery store to stock up. I picked out bottle after bottle of liquor until I had twelve bottles in my shopping cart—and some chips. Shopping complete.

The checkout gal started ringing up the bottles, smiled and said, "Having a party?" Quizzically, I said, "No." I will never forget the look on that woman's face. I remember the utter humiliation I felt as I realized that if I was buying twelve bottles of booze, I should be having a party! I blushed furiously and scurried from the store. I could never shop there again.

That night, I lined up the bottles on the counter and stared my disease in the face. I needed help. I called my friend, Barbara, who sounded pretty excited when I asked if I could go to an AA meeting with her. Apparently, she'd been "saving a seat" for me. When I asked her what tipped her off that I had a problem with alcohol, she said it was the weekend we went to the health spa and I took a six-pack of wine with me. Oh.

At the meeting, I met a wonderful community of people who had faced their demons and were helping others to live life clean and sober. Everyone gave me their phone number and said if I felt like having a drink, to call them instead. I went home and threw away every bottle of alcohol in my house.

They told me I'd have to go to ninety meetings for ninety days. "Are you crazy?" I sputtered. "Have you seen my schedule? Do you know who I am?" Impassive, they shook their heads. "Ninety meetings for ninety days. If you want what we have, you have to do what we do."

"How do you know?" I whined.

"We're sober and you're not," they answered. Well, that made sense.

So I went to their ninety meetings for ninety days. I didn't feel like it. If you wanted alcoholics to feel like going to a meeting before they went to one, the rooms would probably be empty. But as they say, "Suit up and show up." They don't care how you feel about it. Just that you do it.

Old habits die hard, but if you are determined, die they do. I had to face every defect of my character and feel all the feelings that I had used alcohol to avoid. There were nights I cried myself to sleep, looking at the moon deep in the night sky outside my window. "One day," I vowed, "it will be six months from now and I won't hurt this bad."

And one day it was, and I didn't.

Breakdowns will lead eventually to breakthroughs, if you are committed. "It works if you work it." I grew into a new life and a new self. My workshops prospered as I told the raw truth about my experiences. My failures and recovery gave others the courage that they, too, could rise above the past and succeed. My book on money and spirit found a publisher and readers around the world. I cleared away the wreckage of the past and built a better life and a bigger bank account at the same time. Now I have a business I love, work that doesn't feel hard, and clients who praise me and pay me. My recreational beverage of choice is Diet Coke. I have wonderful relationships with family and friends and a spiritual foundation to my life and my work that deepens every day.

Consciously or unconsciously, we create our lives. We choose where we live, who our friends are, what our work is. We choose whether or not we exercise, smoke, take drugs, donate to charity, get a degree, have pets, have spouses, or have children. We pick what we read, what we think, and what we believe. Our lives are testimonials to our choices. Each moment is the point of power. Each moment, we can continue to choose what we have already chosen or we can choose to choose again. A life filled with abundance—inside and out—is ours for the taking.

There is a road from poverty to prosperity, from failure to success. I know, because I have walked it myself. Come.

Chellie C. Campbell

Pause and Reflect

1. Make a list of your addictions and what they are costing you, physically and emotionally. What would it take to eliminate them? Are you prepared to take the first step and ask for help?
2. What activities feed your mind? What activities nourish your body? What activities connect you to your source? Write these down, then choose one in each category and make time for it this week.
3. Go to bed one night in the next week before 10:00 pm (even 9:45). See what kind of impact it makes on the way you think and feel.

LIFE LESSON #5:
CHANGE YOUR MIND

*Change your thoughts and
you change your world.*

NORMAN VINCENT PEALE

Abraham Lincoln once said, "Most folks are about as happy as they make up their minds to be." Was he implying that, when it comes to our happiness, we actually have a choice? Apparently, yes. Research abounds on the impact of positive and negative thinking on ourselves and others, showing that we have the potential to transform ourselves by changing our habits of mind.

For years, it was thought that the brain was fixed and immutable—that we were stuck with what we were born with in terms of our hardware and its abilities. Then along came Sharon Begley's book *Train Your Mind, Change Your Brain*, offering ground-breaking documentation to support the idea that we can even change our brains by changing our thoughts. The results are staggering. These breakthroughs show it is possible to "reset our happiness meter, regain the use of limbs disabled by stroke, train the mind to break cycles of depression and OCD, and reverse age-related changes in the brain."[1]

So where do we start? What needs to be changed about the way we think, anyway? Let's look first at the number and nature of our thoughts. We humans, it seems, have anywhere from 12,000 to 60,000 thoughts per day. But the scary part is that, according to some research, as many as 98 percent of them are exactly the same as we had the day before,[2] and 80 percent are negative. Talk about creatures of habit! And if the mind/body connection is real, it's no wonder we're exhausted at the end of the day—negative thoughts deplete the body by creating corresponding chemicals that weaken the physiology.

So if we can begin to recognize a negative thought— words like "never" and "can't" or anything that diminishes our own or another's sense of self-worth—we can consciously choose to change it. Instead of saying, "I can't meet this deadline," try "I'm not sure how I'm going to meet this deadline, but I'm going to do my best to make it happen."

A large portion of the so-called "negative" thoughts is composed of whining and complaining. Pastor Will Bowen of Christ Church Unity in Kansas City knows well the power of changing the way you think. In an effort to help his congregation find a concrete way to focus on what they *do* want rather than what they *don't* want, he created a purple bracelet and gave one to everyone at church one

Sunday. Because it takes twenty-one days to create a new habit, the idea was for people to switch the bracelet to the other wrist if they found themselves complaining—and keep switching it until they'd gone the full twenty-one days without a single complaint.

The Complaint-Free World Project exploded from 250 bracelets to five million in nine months. Pastor Will receives letters daily from schools, prisons, hospitals, churches, businesses, and even the Pentagon, telling him what a powerful and positive impact the bracelets are having. Families are getting closer. People's health is improving. People are turning their lives around.

Remember: it takes twenty-one days to break a habit and create a new one—not much time and a relatively small commitment. But the results can astonish, as you'll read in the next story by cultural anthropologist Angeles Arrien. Taking responsibility for oneself has a powerful impact on a person and her environment. It is always a step in the direction of wisdom.

The Power of Choice

There was an event in my life that had a very deep impact on me. It is one of the memories I always go back to in meditation, because it's a deep source of inspiration.

I was waiting for the shuttle to take me to the airport. Sitting next to me was this woman reading her newspaper. But my eyes were on a fourteen-year-old boy who was on his skateboard.

He wore his baseball cap turned around with the bill in back, the cool look, you know. And he buzzed us once. He buzzed us twice. Then he came back around a third time for his grand finale, and he inadvertently knocked the newspapers out of the woman's hand.

She immediately started yelling, "Oh, you teenagers! No wonder the world is going to pot, because you're in it! I can't stand it!" And so on.

The boy went down to the corner to talk to his buddy, and they turned back to look at us. Then they talked together some more. In the meantime, she began to roll up her newspaper and get it all back together. She put it under her arm, walked to the middle of the block, and motioned the boy to come over.

Very slowly and reluctantly, he came on his skateboard, and almost as an act of defiance, he turned the baseball cap around, put the bill straight up in front, and said, "Yeah?"

And she said, "What I meant to say is, I was afraid that I would get hurt, and my comments were coming from a place of fear. They weren't right, and I hope that you will accept my apology."

That boy's face has been an inspiration for me ever since, because he looked at her and smiled, then he said, "How cool."

I was deeply moved and touched by that moment.

In Latin America, in some of the Hispanic societies of the world, that moment would be seen as a healing moment, as a holy moment. They would call that moment a *milagro pequeno. Milagro,* miracle. *Pequeno,* small. A small miracle. Within ten minutes time, through conscious awareness, this woman made a choice. She made a life-affirming choice to create a Blessing Way between herself and that boy. A *milagro pequeno.* He will never forget that moment. I will never forget that moment. And she who shapeshifted that moment through conscious choice will not forget that moment.

There comes a time in the spiritual journey when you start making choices from a very different place. One of the most important teachers in my life told me that you know you've touched the beginning of spiritual maturity when you review a choice considering five things: Is this choice in alignment with truth? Is this choice in alignment with health? Is this choice in alignment with happiness? Is this choice in alignment with wisdom? Is this choice in alignment with love?

And if the choice lines up so that it supports truth, health, happiness, wisdom, and love, it's the right choice. That's a choice that indeed furthers life-affirming action and can create the Blessing Way in our own lives as well as other people's lives. Then we have the ultimate experience of being the steward of our new life, and the experience of internal and external success.

Angeles Arrien

Pause and Reflect

1. Write down three versions of "negative thoughts" you have, such as "I can't do_____" or "It's all my fault." Then write down a positive thought you could substitute for each.

2. Participate in the Complaint-Free World Project. Order a purple bracelet from Christ Church Unity and see if you can go twenty-one days without complaining: www.ccunitykc.org.

BECOMING FEARLESS

Courage is not simply one of the virtues, but
the form of every virtue at the testing point.

C. S. Lewis

LIFE LESSON #1:
GROW YOUR COURAGE

If we have no peace, it is because we have
forgotten we belong to one another.

MOTHER TERESA

I've been thinking a lot lately about things that scare me: having to get to the airport in Midwest winter weather when roads are icy; the stock market taking a dive—and my investments with it; realizing my mother is going to die sometime; and that I myself am closer to the end of my life than the beginning.

When I was in my early twenties, I was fearless. My family and friends were aghast when I moved from my hometown of Baton Rouge to Washington, D.C. All that crime!

But crime didn't faze me. My apartment bordered on one of the highest-crime neighborhoods in the city, yet I didn't think twice about walking home from a friend's late at night by myself. Foolish? Possibly. Naïve? Probably. Free? Absolutely. I felt as if I had a radar system in place, an invisible shield of protection and security around me.

Fearlessness served me well in the coming years. I joined the Peace Corps and went to West Africa for two years. I traveled around the world for another year, to exotic—sometimes dangerous—destinations: Yaounde,

Dar es Salaam, the Seychelles. I have faced wild animals in the game parks of East Africa, been victimized by thieves in the streets of Rome, and kidnapped while hitch-hiking across country. I've been trapped underwater, pummeled by unrelenting ocean waves on the West African coast. And I've been stranded in a brutal Midwest snow-storm. Each time, a quiet courage carried me through.

But what do we do when we can't seem to find our courage? We may not be facing wild animals, but still we encounter situations every day that put us in fight-or-flight mode. A siren goes off, signaling that a tornado has been spotted on the ground nearby. A company downsizes and jobs disappear. An ice storm takes out a town's electricity—and the temperature plunges to minus 10 degrees.

A "life partner" suddenly decides to move on. A family member is diagnosed with cancer. Someone close dies, and we don't know how we'll manage life without them. Our youngest child is suddenly ready to leave home, and the joy of seeing her happy about beginning her own life is accompanied by a sense of great loss.

In times like these, we may have to "grow" our courage by reaching out to others. Armed with friends and like-minded advocates, we can regain our sense that we are not alone. So many of us are independent minded. We're capable. We can even keep our terror under wraps, hardly letting others know we're scared. But vulnerability is a powerful place to come from. A kind of grace falls upon us when we understand Helen Keller's words: "When indeed shall we learn that we are all related one to the other, that we are all members of one body?"

This realization would save Pam George's career and impact the lives of children everywhere.

☕ Testing the Sleeping Giant

When I chose my life's work, I knew it would demand that I work hard and be creative, but little did I know that it would also ask me to be brave, really brave. That turned out to be the hard part.

As a professor of educational psychology, my *job* is to train teachers, counselors, and principals to evaluate students and school programs. But my *work* goes well beyond that job. For nearly three decades, my dream has been of schools where students are judged by their performances, and test scores are only a small part of their educational records. I teach about assessments that are less harmful to kids than most standardized IQ, aptitude, or achievement tests. I also document schools' misuses of standardized tests.

My mission began the day my eight-year-old daughter, Kemen, came home from school with tears streaming down her face.

"Momma, I failed the math test!" she cried. "I got the worst score in the class!"

I calmed her down, confident she was mistaken. Kemen had always loved math, breezed through her homework, and tutored other kids in her third-grade class. But as I studied the scores for the standardized end-of-grade test, I saw that she was right. She had scored 6 out of 100—the lowest score of her class!

Because I knew both Kemen's strength in math and the pitfalls of standardized testing, I began to search out the cause of such a questionable result.

I asked to view the exam—denied. I asked for a retest—also denied. I then asked to have her original test scored by hand. It was discovered that the answer sheet had been a photocopy. The scoring machine could not read it accurately and reported a false score.

That was the end of that problem for Kemen. Today she is happily studying applied math and statistics in college. But for me, this experience was only a beginning.

I became committed to helping parents and teachers prevent misuse of standardized tests. I counseled parents whose children were mistakenly labeled mentally handicapped based on IQ scores. I worked with teachers whose good judgment concerning students was often trumped by standardized tests. I observed classes where the curriculum had become "drill and kill" test preparation that bored the kids. And I worked with students whose futures were harmed by exams that underrepresented their abilities.

I knew I had to alert other parents and teachers to the problems I had found with testing, and so I wrote a book about testing our children, the first of many that would call for test reform. I wanted it to be readable, with testing statistics simplified and test questions demystified. It illustrated common errors in testing practices and taught parents about their rights.

The book was reviewed favorably and the first edition sold out. But then a sleeping giant awoke! One of the country's wealthiest test companies sued me. As publisher of a commonly used IQ test, it claimed my book encouraged parents to violate the company's copyright by telling readers about test items hitherto kept confidential. In addition to claims of enormous financial damages, they demanded that my book be withdrawn and that I never write or teach about standardized testing again.

The combative language of the company's New York lawyers stunned me. I was also frightened, for I did not have tenure at my university and this would surely jeopardize my prospects. The company's demand for financial reparations astounded me, for it represented more money than I could earn in a lifetime.

What was I to do? If I caved in to the industry's legal pit

bulls, I would certainly lose my *work*—which provided meaning and a sense of calling. But if I fought back, I would most likely lose my *job*—a professorship for which I had worked hard. For a few days I was so worried that I didn't eat. Night after night, anxious thoughts crowded my mind, and I didn't sleep.

In the small hours of one morning, a ray of light finally broke in. I sat up, suddenly energized by a realization—I was not alone. For years, I had met colleagues around the country who shared my concerns about the misuse of standardized tests. A coalition had developed of like-minded educators and civil-rights advocates, and I needed to call on their support!

I picked up the phone and got started. I called John (the energetic test reform advocate), Diana (the social justice attorney), Bob (the great networker), Page (the smart rural educator), and Chuck (the journalism professor). Each colleague called a few more. By the end of the second day, messages of support were flooding in.

Soon the news reached civil rights groups and universities across the country. My colleagues told a simplified version of my story, that "the large testing industry was trying to set a dangerous precedent for copyright superiority by beating up on a well-meaning teacher from a public university in the South who was unlikely to fight back."

By the end of the week, an education advocacy center

based at Harvard began coordinating my defense. Soon a famous law firm in Washington, D.C., took the case *pro bono*. This team of lawyers chose to fight the case using the First Amendment's safeguarding of the right of a teacher or parent to criticize test materials and practices.

As my battle continued, something strange happened—I started to feel brave! I knew I could stand my ground and did not have to give in to the powerful testing industry. And I did not have to do this all by myself.

We settled the case favorably out of court in a few months. The book again was available for sale, and today I continue to lecture and publish about inappropriate uses of standardized testing.

One day near the end of the deliberations, I was looking around the Washington conference room at the group of powerful advocates from Boston, New York, and D.C. They were colleagues, and now friends, who championed my book and shared my dream of better measures for kids. I felt so grateful for their support, their knowledge, their skills, and their energy. I felt braver than I ever had in my life. And I smiled as I realized that the testing industry had picked on the *wrong* woman!

Pamela George

Pause and Reflect

1. What's going on in your life right now that's making you feel nervous or worried? Ask yourself if it's something you really need to face alone, or whether others might be able to help you. Who could you call on for help?
2. Whom do you recognize as the mentors in your life—those whom you look to for inspiration and support? Can you think of someone older than you whom you could ask to become a mentor for you, in terms of your career, business, personal relationships, etc.?

LIFE LESSON #2:
PRACTICE COMPASSION

It is only with the heart that one can see rightly;
what is essential is invisible to the eye.

I have always wanted to be compassionate, and when I met Mother Teresa, I experienced the embodiment of compassion. It happened while I was traveling around the world in the early seventies. I was staying at the home of a Christian family in Bangalore when my hostess invited me to accompany her to the church she attended to meet "Sister Teresa," as she was still called then. Already world-renowned, Sister Teresa was coming to visit the children in the church's attached orphanage and speak to the women of the church.

I followed Sister Teresa closely around the orphanage, watching her touch and hold the children close, caressing them and speaking to them so lovingly. I tried to follow her example, noticing that it did not come easily to me. Afterwards, she lectured to the group, then stood at the doorway greeting each person.

Suddenly she was holding my hands in hers and looking into my eyes. I have no memory of what she said to me. All I can remember is the feeling of compassion that swept over me and the understanding that I was in the presence of greatness.

Actress Jennifer Claire Moyer says that compassion is not something you do. It's a feeling that arises when you realize that "this river of life that flows through me is the same river of life that flows through everybody and everything that exists." On the other hand, the Dalai Lama talks about *practicing compassion.* "If you want others to be happy, practice compassion. If you want to be happy, practice compassion," he says.

Compassion to me means having a deep awareness of another's suffering without over-identifying with it or being overwhelmed by it ourselves. I don't know if you can go to a seminar and learn how to practice compassion. I try to bring compassion to every action and every relationship, whether personal or professional. Sometimes I'm successful, sometimes I'm not. But although my personality may momentarily forget, my soul does not. And when I am in the presence of compassion, the transmission goes deep into my psyche and my soul, and once again, I become more compassionate.

Mother Teresa often reminded people that we cannot do great things, only small things with great love. Lynne Twist, author of the next story, shows how those small things can have great results.

This story took place just after Lynne had returned from

Africa, where she had been working with the Hunger Project, an international organization she helped found, dedicated to ending hunger worldwide. At their New York office, she attended a meeting on the accomplishments of the region of West Africa where she had been. Feeling deeply related to Africa, especially the women with whom she had worked, she felt proud, thrilled, and fulfilled by the success they had experienced together.

From there she went to Park Avenue for another meeting of a foundation whose board she was also on. It was about the results of their work taking place in the Middle East, which she described as spectacular and moving. She left the meeting feeling blessed and light enough to walk on water. It is at this point that she picks up the story of what happened next.

The New York City Cabdriver

It was a typical hot summer night in New York City. I had just been at a meeting celebrating some successes in humanitarian work I had been involved with in Africa. I was full of inspiration and fulfillment with the experience of making a difference. It was about 9:30 PM when I hailed a cab, which screeched to the curb to pick me up.

Almost as soon as I got into the cab, I realized that I was

in the presence of a very angry young African-American man, full of enormous rage and hatred. He drove as if he wanted to kill someone. He honked at every moving object. From Park Avenue over to Broadway, he cut people off, jammed his cab into small spaces, and was both rude and reckless. I sat frozen in the back seat; I felt I was in the grip of a raging monster.

Suddenly, an Indian taxi driver, a Sikh man with a turban, cut my driver off, and he went into a rage that was deep, horrible, and frightening. He screamed expletives at this guy, who drove away as fast as he could. But when we came to the next red light on Broadway, the same driver was next to us. My angry, monstrous cabdriver opened the door of our cab, went over to the Indian driver and started pounding on the hood of the car. He started screaming at him: "Racist! You Indian drivers! You Pakistanis!" Then he went around to the open window, pulled out a knife and tried to stab the Indian driver. The Indian driver ducked the knife, the light turned green, and he drove away.

My cabdriver then came back to the car, where I was still sitting in the back seat, unable to move. The knife was still in his hands. My heart was pounding. I was sweating profusely, and blood was coursing through my veins. I thought, *Do I scream for the police? Do I try to get out? What do I do?* I had a million thoughts going through my mind, but perhaps the loudest was, *I can be effective in Bangladesh or Africa in empowering people to begin to turn their situation around, but can I walk my talk with this man?*

I stayed in the cab. There was no chance of getting out anyway, because he pulled away abruptly as the light turned green, at 8 zillion miles an hour. He was still screaming and yelling, so I said to him, "Maybe you should pull over and calm down a little bit, and I'll get out." He turned around with the same rage and started yelling at me: "You white honky, you rich, white woman, you have no idea what I've been through in my life. You're just a bunch of . . ." Focused on me now, he hardly looked at the road as he drove. I was frozen with fear as he went on and on.

And then suddenly, I stopped listening from my head, and I moved into a place of compassion in my heart. Somewhere around 42nd Street and Broadway, I just leapt from my head to my heart. I could hear the rage and anger, but also the terror and hurt in his voice. When we got to our destination, which was in Greenwich Village where I was staying, he turned around and screamed the cab fare that I owed him.

Now I don't know if we could scientifically prove this, but when you're in your heart, it seems you have access to courage. I think there's no fear, because love is devoid of fear. I have often heard my mother say that when you drop into your heart, no matter what the situation is, you'll handle it with compassion and wisdom.

I said to him, "You know what? I don't have anywhere else to go now; my day is over. Would you like to talk?"

He looked at me as if I was completely crazy. He stopped yelling. He stared at me for a moment and then, slowly, started talking. He started telling me the tragic and brutal story of his life. He talked about his mother, who was a drug addict on crack, and his father, who had beaten him and kicked him in his stomach when he was three years old, which had given him problems with his back ever since. He talked about the horrors of his neighborhood.

Suddenly, I realized that I could no longer separate myself from this man. I realized, *He and I are just the same. His world is the world I live in, too.*

And I got out of the back seat and into the front and took his hand. Right beneath our hands was the knife. The switchblade was still open. Then he started to cry. He started weeping about the horrors of his life, and the Pakistani cabdrivers, and Indian cabdrivers—he insulted every single group completely and totally. But this time it was in communication with me, rather than yelling at someone.

By the time he finished his story, he was sobbing. I took his other hand and looked at him. I told him my name was Lynne, and he told me his name was Richard. I said thank you; he said thank you. I paid him and got out of the cab.

Again, in that moment, I realized that we are all part of the same human condition. I saw that even in this angry man, the yearning to love and be loved was at the heart of who he was. I had been given a deep understanding of how the human spirit can be crushed and moved to rage. I could actually feel it in my heart.

I don't know if it made a difference in this man's life. I don't know if he went on to murder the next person he picked up. But I maintained my own integrity. I walked my talk and it wasn't in Bangladesh or sub-Saharan Africa, where I'm supposed to walk my talk. It was in New York, where the norm would have been to get out of there as fast as possible and report the guy. I don't know what came over me, but somehow I brought love and compassion and myself to him.

I feel that this man is a part of my life forever. To this day, I have love for him—and I believe that makes a difference. I can't prove it, and I have no evidence. I'll probably never see him again. But I really believe that because I've taken a stand to give my life in a way that makes a difference, every action I take can, in fact, make a difference and generate a more compassionate and loving world.

Gandhi said, "The unadulterated love of one person can nullify the hatred of millions." I think that is true. I believe that when you take a stand with your life—powerful enough, grand enough, blessed enough—you will always find the way to your heart and moments of truth.

Lynne Twist

Pause and Reflect

1. With three people you come in touch with today, see if you can listen from your heart, rather than your head. This means trying to feel what they're saying rather than focusing solely on the words.
2. Close your eyes for a few minutes. See if you can call up the feeling of compassion.
3. Now think of someone close to you who's suffering or challenged by something big right now. Can you be aware of and sensitive to his or her situation without making it your own?

Life Lesson #3:
Surrender to "What Is"

Surrender is giving up control but not losing power.

Sondra Ray

I had just returned from a ten-day working vacation in Florida. I would have only two days at home before driving to Chicago for a business conference. The plan was to unpack; do laundry; repack; go through mail, e-mail, and phone messages; and pay bills. I also had it in the back of my mind to squeeze in a little writing on this book.

The first thing I noticed when I drove in the driveway was that my grass was several inches tall. I had gotten the message while gone that the lawn had a fungus and needed to be treated before being cut, and I had made some calls to try to have things taken care of before I got home. Apparently, nothing had been done yet, and both grass and fungus were clearly getting out of control.

Inside, the refrigerator was leaking; I couldn't reach my normally accessible neighborhood repairman. My printer wouldn't work; I couldn't reach my normally accessible computer man. I went to an appointment, only to find that they were running so far behind that they couldn't see me. I went to the grocery store, where I quickly discovered that I had left my list at home.

There's more, but you get the point. Who hasn't had days like this? Of course, these "problems" are completely insignificant when viewed in light of the plight of people struggling for survival in many countries. But, to paraphrase Mother Teresa, God puts you in the life you have, and whether you find yourself in a palace or the street, you accept that. It seems ironic that however comfortable our circumstances, we seem to find plenty of ways to be challenged by them!

What can you do when nothing seems to be going right? As the Borg on *Star Trek* say: "Resistance is futile." The frustration I feel in a situation like this comes only when it's not okay to let things be just as they are—or when I think I have the power to change them and I don't. The only way to experience peace in times like these is to surrender to "what is." It's not easy, especially if you are strong-willed—like someone I saw in the mirror this morning.

But it seems to me that the events I described here might well have been signposts for me to stop trying so hard. I undoubtedly would have been better off adopting a more leisurely pace getting back from vacation, perhaps doing a little writing and letting go of my obsession that bills and the lawn and all my e-mails couldn't wait until I got back from Chicago. When I really examined things, the only thing that absolutely *had* to be taken care of immediately was the refrigerator—and there was still time for that before I had to leave. It was a classic example of creating problems for myself by thinking that life needed to look and be a certain way—my way.

In our culture, surrender often implies giving up or giving in; we tend to view it as weakness. But I believe there are times when surrendering is the most powerful action (or nonaction) a person can take. This doesn't mean using surrender as an excuse for apathy or to avoid being responsible. Surrender in this case means to let go completely of outcomes. If we can do this, even for a split second, we allow an opening in which the cosmic flow of life takes over, transforming frustration, anger, or fear into a deep trust in something greater than ourselves.

And, as you will see in the following story by Ciella Kollander, it could even mean a whole new life.

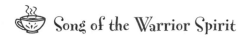 Song of the Warrior Spirit

My parents were singers and musicians, and my entire life has been filled with music. From the age of four I studied piano, voice, dance, accordion, and violin, and by seven I was singing radio commercials.

My father was a minister, and we would sing for prison inmates and hospital patients. I sang for our troops, too. During World War II, whenever my mother and I traveled from

San Diego to Virginia to visit family, the trains were full of troops who delighted in having me sing and dance for them.

When I was sixteen we moved to the Philippines, where my father was administrator at the Allied Officer's training school. Radio and music were still the joy of my life. I befriended the DJs at the base radio station and ended up having my own R&B show.

After college, I married and moved to Las Vegas, where I performed as a singer and dancer at many hotels. I shared the stage with performers such as Elvis and comedian Don Rickles, and I had coffee between shows with Dan Rowan and Dick Martin from television's *Laugh-In,* two of my funniest friends.

When my husband and I split up, I moved to Los Angeles, where I became a singer and contractor for several of the major studios. My life was filled with hard work, but lots of glamour too. Andy Williams, The Osmonds, Bobby Darin, Paul Horn, Chad & Jeremy, John Davidson, country star Lee Greenwood, and jazz greats Roger Kellaway and Tom Scott—I collaborated, performed, and toured with them all.

By this time, it was the sixties. My success seemed unstoppable, almost magical. I became a staff songwriter for A&M Records, with a studio of my own at the old Charlie Chaplin Studios. A song I cowrote there was selected by The Fifth Dimension for their *Aquarius* album, which went platinum.

Like so many "flower children" of the sixties, I learned how to meditate. I loved it so much that I trained to become a meditation teacher. I moved to Carmel, where I hung out with people like Jill St. John, Clint Eastwood, and friends. My life was beautiful. I was teaching meditation and felt like I was in the lap of the divine. Little did I know that all that was about to change.

On December 27, 1974, I was driving to a meeting in the Bay area. It was 11:30 in the morning, and as it began to drizzle, the highway became slippery.

I lost control of the car, which spun across the median into oncoming traffic. I was hit head-on and thrown into a railing, which stopped me from going over the embankment into the canyon below. It was serious.

The first thing I realized after the collision was that my consciousness was leaving through the top of my head. I was in a huge field of light and was filled with a palpable bliss beyond description. I watched the mechanics of the universe as it calculated the unfathomable equation of my destiny. I became aware—without thinking—that I had not finished my job as mother or teacher. I watched the decision being made—yes, I would come back.

From far away I heard a moan and felt a deep compassion. As I was drawn back into my physical body, I realized that the moan was coming from me.

I should have been dead by the time the ambulance arrived. Two main arteries had been severed, and I had probably lain there for an hour by the time help arrived.

I heard someone say, "We're going to have to get a torch." When they finally blow-torched me out of the wreckage and carried me to the ambulance, I was slipping between life and death.

My injuries were devastating. The left side of my skull was crushed, as were my right elbow and arm, and my liver. My right lung had collapsed, and the bones in my ribcage were sticking through my skin and my clothes. When I reached the hospital, even orderlies were fainting from the sight. I had approximately ninety fractures, and the doctors considered amputating my arm. But worse than everything was this: my vocal cords, trachea, and esophagus had been virtually destroyed.

As the doctors performed the surgeries, I saw gorgeous hands of light dancing over the center of my body, the long, graceful fingers reweaving what looked like an intricate snowflake of light. Through it all, even though at times I appeared to have no vital signs, I remained fully awake inside and aware of everything.

After the surgeries, the doctors told me that I would never talk, much less sing, again. I thought, *If I can't sing, I don't want to live.* There was only one thing I could do: surrender.

This was something I had been forced to do all my life, so I was well prepared. All the best things that had happened to me—my music, giving birth, traveling the world alone, facing huge audiences that both thrilled and terrified me—happened because I was willing to walk through the fear and surrender to the moment, to the unknown, and to my own dreams.

Now my life had changed irrevocably, and I was being asked to surrender more deeply. I had lost my voice, which was my love and my career, and which I had taken for granted. I didn't know if I would recover, and yet surrender kept bringing me an unspeakable bliss, like a river of liquid love.

I meditated almost constantly, and I began composing a love song to God in my head. I was in a constant state of awe and gratitude.

The miracles continued. Occasionally a sound would escape from my vocal cords. I was out of the hospital in only five weeks. Everyone was astonished. The doctors said I'd gone beyond anything they had learned in medical school.

I spent the next year resting, meditating, exercising, and studying. During that time, my voice began to return, and approximately 200 surgeons, doctors, nurses, and therapists started meditating because of what they had seen happen to me. I taught many of them myself. Several hospitals had conferences about my case, at which I was able to speak personally about my experiences.

Thirty years later, I am still healing, but life is good. I am writing, coaching performers, and composing and recording once again. To my delight, I have recovered more than four out of five-and-a-half octaves of my former vocal range.

As a result of my accident, I know that death is not something to be afraid of. It's full of light, full of love. I'm no longer afraid to die—or to live. I also have more patience, compassion, and willingness to accept things as they are. My values have changed, and although I travel the world teaching, I make my home in a small town where I tend my garden, ride my bicycle, and teach young people in the local performing arts conservatory.

I sometimes have regrets, and yet today I am creating the best music of my life. When I was a child, I thought I had to be on life's big, glittering stages, but life is simpler now. I have finally gotten to the music in me that feels like real medicine for the soul—the true purpose of art and music.

Ciella Kollander

Pause and Reflect

1. Learn the Serenity Prayer:

   God, grant me the serenity
   To accept the things I cannot change,
   The courage to change the things I can,
   And the wisdom to know the difference.

2. Use it often.

3. What are you concerned about today? Ask yourself, Is this something within my power to change? If the answer is no, drop it.

Life Lesson #4:
Recognize What's Real

*To live with fear and not be afraid
is the final test of maturity.*

Edward Weeks

Meryl, whose story appears in this book, sums up her business of teaching people how to "speak strong" with these words: "Say what you mean, mean what you say, and don't be mean when you say it."

I'm working on the "mean what you say" part right now; I'm trying to make sure my language fits my reality. Of course, in order to do this, I have to be clear what the truth actually is—in other words, recognize what's real. It's not truthful to say, for example, "I can't afford it," if the more accurate truth is that I can afford it, but just choose not to buy it. It may seem subtle, but this exercise is helping me to become more aware of my feelings and to connect with others more honestly. It's also helping me clean up my relationship with money.

Sometimes we invent things to be afraid of. We hear that our company is downsizing and immediately panic—even though we have no facts and don't really know which jobs will be affected. Sometimes we expect the worst, hoping we're wrong and secretly thinking how good we'll feel if disaster doesn't strike. It's like telling someone you're sure you've failed the test, then making an A.

The opposite can also be true: Reality can be worse than we're willing to accept. A woman went through bankruptcy, then optimistically started another business. However, she couldn't bring herself to spend within her income, and ended up in a second bankruptcy. In this case, failure to recognize what was real seems to have resulted in denial.

Sometimes old habits make it hard to realize that the truth has changed for us. An interesting example is the woman who recently attended an open house given by friends who had just moved into their new home. On the way home, she and her husband starting comparing themselves to their friends, asking themselves why they didn't have a home like that. But when they examined the reality of the situation, they realized that they loved their home, and they really didn't want what their friends had (including the hefty mortgage).

In the following story, Linda Elliott was used to working in an environment where the prevalent response to problems seemed based on the biological response to protect and defend oneself—even at the expense of others. So often this kind of response can escalate in our emotions and minds to the point where the "fight-or-flight" response is not appropriate, simply based on something we've made up. Linda shows us how stepping back from emotions and imagination allowed her to recognize what was real—and the dramatic change in her corporate culture that resulted.

☕ Running with the Bulls

When I arrived at work that morning, it clearly wasn't business as usual at Visa International. People were moving about quickly, looking grim, and the air was thick with tension. Someone told me the news: we had had a three-minute card-servicing outage during the night.

Visa International operates the systems that process about two-thirds of all credit card transactions worldwide. If you use a credit card to buy a snorkel in Tahiti or rent a car in New Zealand, chances are Visa International will verify and approve the transaction. When the systems for real-time verification of cards were originally set up, it was groundbreaking. For the first time consumers could charge purchases in any currency, anywhere, and the banks that issued the cards could verify whether the card was valid.

Such dramatic changes are not brought to market by timid people. Visa International was full of bold, dynamic, forceful professionals who knew their market and their technology. To succeed in this environment, you had to run with the bulls.

I had been at Visa only a few months and was one of the

newer managers controlling these systems. Every morning at eight o'clock we had a "flash" meeting to discuss every systems event from the previous twenty-four hours. When the entire system experienced a failure, no matter how small, the team had to determine what had happened, how to correct it, and how to prevent it from ever happening again.

These actions were undertaken with the utmost urgency. A system outage of a minute was considered a near catastrophe. An outage of over two minutes could result in people losing their jobs and systems undergoing major overhauls. During an outage, merchants get no response when they swipe a card through their terminals—and they ask the buyer if he or she has another card. The result is a loss of revenue for both Visa and the banks that issue the cards. Worse, cardholders tend to put a card that has been declined at the back of their wallets, never to be used again.

As I sat through the flash meeting, I felt terror rising in my chest. This three-minute outage seemed to have been caused, at least in part, by the components for which I was responsible. That awful fact put me in charge of a task force that would determine the root cause of the issue and then take whatever action was necessary.

An hour later, at the first task force meeting, I found myself at the head of a long table packed with twenty-five grim-faced, determined, and powerful people, most of whom had been doing this for years. All but one were men. This was the mideighties and it didn't seem odd to me that there weren't more women at the table.

I felt my male coworkers treated women fairly but doubted we had the required toughness. The people around the table wanted answers, but also, in many cases, they were determined to place the root cause anywhere but in their own areas. This disaster was both an opportunity and a threat to every manager. The corporate culture was such that any blood in the water brought out the sharks. When something went wrong, people would try to find someone to pin the blame on. If you were struck a serious blow, everyone jumped on you in an often career-ending "shark attack." At this meeting, I knew the sharks were circling.

Everyone was looking intently at me. What a target I was—new to the company, younger than most, and a woman! I knew they thought I should be easy to control and run right over. I'm sure they expected me to be in tears any minute, and it was true that inside I was terrified. I knew my job was on the line, but outwardly I remained calm. I knew that I must be strong, but I also knew that I must be careful and fair. I could accept the concept of running with the bulls, but attacking with the sharks didn't work for me.

I took a breath and began to speak. I told these strong and determined people that we had to have the full story, and that nothing would be overlooked. Then I said the unthinkable, that if the problem was in my area, I would accept that and deal with it, and I expected the same of others. We would go by the facts, fix the problems, and not look for scapegoats. This was a problem we could solve together. In short, I said I would not stand for any game playing, second-guessing, or personal attacks.

When I finished speaking, the room was quiet. I had surprised everyone with this open, straightforward approach. Then I outlined the steps we needed to take. I suggested that we adjourn and get the information needed for the next meeting.

As we left the room, everyone seemed relieved. From that day forward, I was accepted as a straight player, powerful and worth listening to. My simple, straightforward strategy worked. We found that there were several things that contributed to the problem. My group was the source of some faults, but so were several others. We all put forward our plans to fix the issues in our own areas and then worked together to refine those plans. We created a model for a new way of dealing with these crises. There was no blood in the water and no flashing of sharp teeth.

Within a few years, outages on the Visa systems became virtually nonexistent. For one period of five years there were no outages at all. This is a world-class company, and I feel honored to have been a part of it. I stayed at Visa for fourteen years, eventually becoming an executive vice president. It was a great place to work and to learn how women can have a positive influence in a corporate culture.

One of the most significant things we can bring to the workplace is the understanding that fear isn't necessary in the exercise of power. People can run with the bulls, but they don't need to attack with the sharks. The committed efforts of good people are more than enough to achieve great things.

Linda Elliott

Pause and Reflect

1. Consider again what's making you afraid or nervous right now. Ask yourself whether this concern is based on fact or conjecture—something that might happen in the future. If it's still speculation at this point, practice saying Atticus Finch's words from To Kill a Mockingbird: "It's not time to worry yet."
2. What is the "story" you are telling yourself about what is happening in your life? What is the reality?

LIFE LESSON #5:
BE PRESENT

This place where you are right now,
God circled on a map for you.

HAFIZ

I was going through one of the darkest periods of my life. The man I thought I was going to marry—my soul mate— had just ended our relationship. To make matters worse, I worked for him. Since his office was separated from the rest of us by a wall with a huge window, there was no escaping his expressions and body language that told me whenever he was on the phone with another woman.

I was devastated. I could hardly breathe at moments, my heart felt so crushed. I implored him to let me take my office computer home to work, so I wouldn't be faced with the pain of seeing him every day. He agreed, and the change of venue definitely helped.

But what helped me the most was the advice that a dear friend gave me. First, if I was going to survive, the most important thing was to go to bed every night before 10:00. I knew from my study of health that every hour of sleep we get before midnight is worth two hours after that time.[1] I also knew that staying rested is by far the most effective way to deal with stress. Anyone who's ever gotten up in the morning without having had enough sleep knows how hard life can be when we're tired. When challenges are accompanied by fatigue, we can feel hopeless.

The second thing I needed to do was to focus on the things I had to be grateful for. Every night before falling asleep, I started writing down at least five good things that had happened to me that day. The principle is simple: when we focus on darkness, we usually allow ourselves to be taken deeper and deeper into darkness. When we focus on light—all the good that's in our lives—we attract more and more light.

It is a powerful truth: *Whatever you put your attention on grows stronger in your life.* It's no surprise that when we focus on the negative, that's all we can see. How often have you had ten great things happen to you in your day, but when a friend asks you how it's going, you immediately tell her about the one thing that didn't go so well? As someone has said, "The more you believe something *matters,* the more solid and tangible it becomes."

Sometimes we get so involved thinking about the past or the future that we simply forget what's going on right in front of us. At times like these, I find it valuable to remember the advice of my friend Stacy, whose life was turned upside down when her husband left her with their three sons. She couldn't figure out what was going to happen down the road, but she knew her children would be home from school for lunch. So she put a sign on her refrigerator that said, "Just make lunch." She calls it training for living in the moment and adds, "There's no knowing what the crystal ball holds, but every outcome starts with 'making lunch.'"

This is what happened to Ellen Greene in the next story. A classics professor who reads ancient Greek, she has had a longstanding love affair with Greece—which makes the struggle she experienced in the first part of her story surprising. But fortunately, one of her beloved Greek poets got through to her! A shift in the focus of her attention brought her into the present and allowed Ellen to reevaluate her circumstances, transforming a miserable reality into a glorious one.

Her story reminds me of one of my favorite Japanese poems: "My barn having burned to the ground, I can now see the moon."

My Odyssey

I sat at the bus station in Nafplion wishing I'd never gone to Greece in the first place. For three days I had wandered through the city's crooked streets, taking in its Venetian-style buildings, busy markets, and colorful wharf, a curious mixture of foreign tourists and local fishermen fixing their tangled nets. Newly divorced, I was proud to have been bold enough to travel by myself outside the United States for the first time in my life.

In retrospect it seems crazy to think that traveling alone to a country I'd never seen, only imagined, would give me any solace. But for years, as a graduate student at Berkeley, I'd studied the ancient texts of Greek literature. The visual images of ruined Greek temples and the sounds and smells of the poetic landscapes of Sappho's poetry had evoked a powerful longing in me. These places, I imagined, could offer the safe haven I was looking for.

But my stay in Nafplion hadn't worked out that way. Since I had arrived in the busy harbor town, all I could see were couples walking hand in hand, arm in arm. They were all happy, I thought. I felt so far from them as I sat in the town square, writing in my journal, trying to stave off intense feelings of loneliness.

Now, as I waited to catch a boat to the island of Paros, I felt utterly defeated. Although this place was beautiful, being here only made me feel worse, not better. All I could see was a parade of happy couples passing in front of me. I just wanted to get out of here. In desperation, I reached for my copy of C. P. Cavafy's poems from inside my bag. In those days I carried several books of poetry with me everywhere I went, and this modern Greek poet was one of my favorites.

I immediately came upon his poem "Ithaca." It uses

Odysseus' long journey home to Ithaca from the battle-fields of Troy to convey that life is a journey full of adventure, if we are open to it. Something in me changed profoundly as words jumped out at me:

"When you set out on your journey to Ithaca, pray that the road is long, full of adventure, full of knowledge. . . . That the summer mornings are many, when, with such pleasure, with such joy you will enter ports seen for the first time; stop at Phoenician markets, and purchase fine merchandise, mother-of-pearl and coral, amber and ebony, and sensual perfumes of all kinds . . . visit many Egyptian cities, to learn and learn from scholars. Always keep Ithaca in your mind. . . . But do not hurry the voyage at all. It is better to let it last for many years; and to anchor at the island when you are old, rich with all you have gained on the way, not expecting that Ithaca will offer you riches. Ithaca has given you the beautiful voyage."[2]

I was stunned. I was well aware of the saying: "It's the journey, not the destination." But this poem evoked with such immediacy the possibility of "the journey." There I was, longing for the future and blinded by the past, when my life was happening right in front of me. I needed to wake up, to view everything as "ports seen for the first time"—that is what had eluded me. I put the book down, feeling that now I could go forward, alone, to welcome whatever came.

And, indeed, life became magical. Feeling like an ancient epic warrior, I boarded the ship and sailed deck class to the island of Paros. That night I lay sleepless, dazzled by the conjunction of stars, sea air, and the odd assortment of people trying to sleep on deck under the blaze of bright lights. After several hours on bumpy roads, the next morning, with Greek music blaring from the bus driver's tape player, we arrived at the small fishing village of Aliki. All the rooms in the village were booked, but I convinced the hotel manager to let me sleep in a tiny, windowless room on the roof.

For a week I prowled Aliki's dusty streets, tested out my new swimming skills in the crystal clear water, and talked with Greeks over muddy Greek coffee and ouzo. Every afternoon, after hours of talking, swimming, and walking along the harbor, I went up to my roof, a cup of thick Greek coffee in hand. There I sat while the wind came up, snapping the towels and sheets on the line, even knocking flowers off their stems. I had never felt a wind like that. It was relentless. But I sat content, happy to be in its path.

After a week on Paros I sailed to Crete, hungry for my next adventure. At dawn I arrived at Iraklion, Crete's capital, and the next day traveled to nearby Knossos to see the ancient temples and palaces, remains of the earliest known Western civilization. The reconstructed ruins of this palace at Knossos drew me into its ancient secrets. I wasn't prepared for the brilliant reds, blues, and golds of their wall paintings, or the faces that seemed to stare out at me from those walls. As I stood in the queen's bedroom, the remnants of her bathtub sitting there, a monument to the intimacies shared by women through time, my mind came alive with images of these people as they carried on the business of life. I walked past rows and rows of pottery shards, broken columns, and fragments of stone, potent with life.

I walked outdoors and stood amid the olive trees, the cicadas shrieking from their unseen places, and I knew I was home. I could see the water of the ancient Mediterranean in the distance, glistening in the late-afternoon sun. I was comforted to know that Homer's wine-dark sea was still here. And I was here too—fully present and able to receive the many gifts of my "beautiful voyage."

Ellen Greene

Pause and Reflect

1. Notice what's going on around you right now. How do you feel? Are you thirsty? Need a bathroom break? Do you like your surroundings, or would you prefer something different? Do you need to take a quick walk to get the kinks out of your neck from sitting at a desk for a while? Do you need a few minutes alone to regain some silence and equanimity?

2. Later today or this week, try to evaluate the truth of your present situation and circumstances. Then take action if you'd like to change something and it feels appropriate. Even just noticing can be a wonderful place to begin practicing being in the present.

HOLDING HANDS, BUILDING BRIDGES

It's kind of fun to do the impossible.

Walt Disney

LIFE LESSON #1:
LET LOVE LEAD

Help thy brother's boat across, and lo!
Thine own has reached the shore.

HINDU PROVERB

They say that laughter is the best medicine. But love is the greatest healer of them all.

I had just given a presentation for a client company on the Gulf Coast. It was a deeply connecting experience for everyone present, and the audience was still applauding as I walked off the stage and over to my purse to grab a pen, before being whisked to the back of the room to autograph books.

As I turned toward the back of the hall, a woman came up to me and opened and closed her mouth several times, as if she wanted to say something but couldn't. When she finally spoke, she told me that I had really messed up her plans. Confused, I asked what she meant. She told me that she had been planning to commit suicide the next night, but that now, after hearing me speak, she was going to have to rethink everything.

I took her hand and looked deeply into her eyes. I knew that far more than what I had said, this woman had felt and received the transmission of love that had been so palpable in the room, generated not only by me, but also by everyone present. This love had healed, as love always does.

But *how* does love heal exactly? It's the mind/body/spirit connection again. When the heart is touched, chemicals responsible for good health and a sense of well-being are released in the body. Research has found that when a person is a recipient of an act of kindness, his or her serotonin levels increase, strengthening the immune system. But interestingly, the serotonin level also increases in the person *performing* the act of kindness, strengthening his or her immune system as well. And amazingly, if someone simply witnesses an act of kindness performed by another, he or she also experiences the same physiological results and benefits![1]

The story you are about to read is about medicine, the kind that helps the sick and injured. But it is first about love, and what happens when love leads. In this story, love provides the clarity, the opening, and the grace for a miracle to happen.

Don't Take No for an Answer

For many years it has been my privilege to play a role in bringing relief to thousands of people around the world who have been hit by natural disasters. Through the support of my family and Sarasota Sunrise Rotary Club Foundation, I have worked with earthquake victims in Iran, hurricane survivors in Florida and Mississippi, and brave souls in Sri Lanka and Indonesia in the wake of the 2004 tsunami.

On October 8, 2005, ten months after the disaster, I was on my way once again to Indonesia and Sri Lanka on another post-tsunami relief mission. Sitting in the transit lounge at Dubai International Airport, I suddenly heard on the news that an earthquake registering 8.6 on the Richter scale had just occurred in Pakistan.

My thoughts immediately went back to the destruction I had witnessed in Iran, where the 6.6 earthquake had claimed the lives of 40,000 people. Now, with this news about Pakistan, I knew instantly that there would be a greater need for my services and expertise there than in Indonesia, where relief efforts had been continuing for ten months. I was carrying $150,000 worth of medicine with me—and the experience to use it wisely.

Without taking another second to evaluate the situation, I went to the ticket counter and bought a ticket for Pakistan. Then, because I am a Rotarian, I called the governor of the Pakistani Rotary Club to notify him of my arrival.

When I landed in Lahore, the airport was teeming with arrivals waiting to get through Immigration. My request to be taken to the immigration office was granted immediately, but my hopes were short-lived. After thumbing through my passport twice, the immigration officer informed me that I could not enter his country: I did not have a visa.

I was aghast. I told him about my experience with disaster relief. I told him about the $150,000 worth of medicine, drugs, sutures, and splints I had with me. I explained, cajoled, and tried to reason with the man. But to no avail. After being detained for two hours, my patience wearing thin, I was told repeatedly that there was nothing they could do. It was the law.

It was unthinkable to me that I was standing there with so much to offer—and nothing but red tape standing between those desperate people and me. I remained undeterred. I asked to speak to the Duty Office at the Foreign Ministry, who repeated what everyone else had told me: their hands were tied; they could do nothing because of the law. Suddenly, something prompted me to ask him, "Who has written this law: God or man?" After some thought, he admitted that man had written the law, to which I promptly replied, "If man has written this law, not taking into account the possibility of an 8.6 earthquake, then man can change the law."

There was a small opening. The officer asked me what I thought he should do. "Change the law," I said, "to permit anyone who arrives who has the expertise to help you to be granted a visa on entry. Then thank them profusely, offer them a cup of tea, and send them on their way to save a life or two!"

I got my visa. Along with the global community of Rotarians who joined me in my mission to help the victims, I was one of the first international aid workers in Pakistan. We worked in some of the most devastated areas, where sliding mountains had destroyed roads and whole villages, burying thousands alive. Over 7,600 schools were destroyed, taking with them as many as 96 percent of their students and teachers.

Since that trip, I have returned to Pakistan four times on follow-up relief missions and delivered more than $1,000,000 of aid. As with every disaster area, the need is great and long-term, yet it is my honor to play even a small part.

Oh yes—and that law about the visas? It was changed the morning after my infamous encounter with Immigration, allowing anyone arriving in Pakistan to help to be given a visa on entry. I am so grateful that I never take no for an answer!

Ali Tahiri

Pause and Reflect

What has your heart been calling you to do lately? Have you been wanting to pick up a card for a co-worker who's been down in the dumps? Would you like to spend extra time with your kids this weekend? Carve out the time to do it. Put it on your calendar if necessary.

LIFE LESSON #2:
START WHERE YOU ARE

I am larger, better than I thought;
I did not know I held so much goodness.

WALT WHITMAN

There's a lovely story by Jaroldeen Asplund Edwards about a woman who planted one of the most beautiful displays of daffodils ever seen, high up on a mountain peak surrounding her small A-frame home. There were five acres of flowers planted in "majestic, swirling patterns— great ribbons and swaths of deep orange, white, lemon yellow, salmon pink, saffron, and butter yellow."

A poster on the patio of her home read: "Answers to the Questions I Know You Are Asking." The first was "50,000 bulbs." The second answer was, "One at a time, by one woman, two hands, two feet, and very little brain." The third answer was, "Began in 1958." Planting one bulb at a time, year after year for more than forty years, this woman had created something of indescribable magnificence, beauty, and inspiration.[1]

Mother Teresa would often exhort people to "just begin." Her home for the dying began when she picked up one woman from the streets of Calcutta. "If I hadn't picked up that one, maybe I wouldn't have picked up the other 40,000," she said.

Starting "where I was" was a lifeline for me when I was earning my living as a technical writer. I often felt overwhelmed when I asked myself, *How will I ever write this manual?* But my boss would gently remind me to look at my project plan and focus on the chapter or section scheduled to be written that day. Just that, nothing more.

How about you? Are you waiting for things to be perfect before you take a step in the direction of your dreams? Waiting for your kids to finish college before you start your own business? Perhaps you could do five minutes of online research this evening, after work. Waiting to take that writing seminar before you start on that book you know is in you? Get up a few minutes earlier tomorrow morning and write about what you see out your window.

Vicky Edmonds "started" in the car on her way to her son's preschool, when she told him about the hurricane that had just struck the Caribbean, where they were planning to vacation. A simple idea led her to take one step, after another, after another.

Try it. Take a step, just one step. Start where you are right now.

Somebody Should Do Something

I was a young mom without a clue how to be one. My husband, Ken, was working for a subsidiary of Holland

America, the cruise company, while I was mostly staying at home with our four-and-a-half-year-old son, Lucas, and newborn son, Ean. But like that of many young moms, my world was small—consistent with the life I had grown up with. That suited me fine because, deep inside, I felt I had nothing to give anybody.

However, I always delighted to break out of my world to go on our annual cruise, which was one of the employee benefits at Ken's company. Our application to go in September 1988 had been accepted, and we were thrilled to be taking our children on a Caribbean cruise to Cozumel, Mexico, and the islands of Grand Cayman and Jamaica.

But four weeks before our departure, Jamaica was struck by Hurricane Gilbert, called by some the biggest storm of the century. I watched in horror TV footage of a five-year-old girl with tears in her eyes, sitting on the steps of a building as water rushed by in the streets. She couldn't find her family, and she couldn't get anywhere. The news report said that all the water was contaminated, and the people were cut off from food supplies. A state of emergency had been declared.

The image of that little girl moved me to tears. As a child, I had felt abandoned too, so my heart was completely with her. I thought, *Somebody should do something to help these people!* This was immediately answered with another thought, *I wonder if I'm somebody?*

It was one of those lucid moments when suddenly there's an opening. I saw a possibility of what I might do, even if it was small. Even a small something might be something. It was terrifying even to think that I might try. What would happen if people laughed at me? But I thought, *I'm going to try.*

The next day as I drove Lucas to school, I told him about Hurricane Gilbert and said, "Why don't we ask all your friends to bring a canned good to school to send to the people who don't have any food."

Lucas's teacher okayed the plan, so I sent a note home with each of the fourteen children in the class. Over the next week, the children excitedly brought in their canned goods. Everybody wants to feel they can give something valuable, and this was the first contribution many of them had ever made.

One of the moms couldn't get to the store, so she sent a $50 check, which enabled me to buy several large cans of food and dried foods in bulk. But how would I send it all? Our income had been cut in half because I was staying home with my newborn child. More checks arrived from parents. They were all talking about it. I finally decided just to keep some of the money for postage, because I couldn't afford to send everything myself.

I was calling UPS and the airlines to find out the cost of

shipping canned goods to Jamaica when a writer from the *Seattle Times* called. He'd heard I was collecting food for the children of the hurricane, and he wrote a small article in the newspaper. Suddenly people started coming to our house to donate food. One woman and her son drove up in a beat-up old pick-up filled with bags of food. When they pulled up, tears started streaming down my face. The woman shook my hand and said, "God bless you."

I had thought I was going to be sending $20 worth of food, and now we could barely walk through the house because there were bags and boxes everywhere.

I called the airlines. Some of them could get the food to Florida, but it was going to cost a fortune—and I didn't have a clue how we'd then get it to Jamaica.

But the week before we were to leave, everything started to fall into place. Eastern Airlines told us they'd ship the food as far as Florida—for free! I was told how to package it and how to fill out the paperwork. We borrowed a truck and made a couple of trips to the airport, where the food was put on a pallet and weighed—we had collected 1,454 pounds of food!

Then, miracle of miracles, Holland America said we could take it with us on our cruise from Florida to Jamaica. Yes, we were still going there. Cruise lines visit the places on planned tours even when they've been affected by a natural disaster. With 1,500 people on board, the tourism can contribute significantly to the rebuilding of a stricken area.

The cruise was fantastic. But we hit our next hurdle when we arrived in Jamaica and the customs agents asked us where the food should be delivered. I had no idea! The agents told us that if we couldn't give them an address by 5:00, they'd have to seize our shipment.

A man standing nearby overheard the conversation and told us about a church that was housing forty children who had lost their homes. We got in the man's car, and he drove wildly for about twenty minutes to the church. The minister was too busy to help, but a missionary there from Minnesota volunteered to pick up the goods with the help of the teenage boys from the church.

We returned to the ship and waited nervously until, just before customs closed at 5:00, the missionary arrived with the boys and a big truck. After loading up the truck, they thanked us profusely and assured us the food would go to help children. Watching that truck drive away, I was dazed, trying to believe it had all worked.

Back in vacation mode, Ken and I decided to tour the island before we left. There was devastation everywhere. Roofs were blown off and broken glass was all over the place, but major reconstruction had already begun. Even as we continued our cruise to other spots on the tour, the feeling of having been a part of something bigger than ourselves stayed with us.

About three weeks after we got home, I learned that our donation had been divided equally between the church housing the children, an orphanage, and a hospital where mothers had given birth prematurely due to the stress of the hurricane. It had all gone to children! I thought about how no one had come to help me when I was a child. But I had exposed the myth that one person alone can do nothing. I had had a lot of help along the way, but taking that first step by myself had healed something in my heart.

I had felt that somebody should do something, and I had turned out to be that somebody.

Vicky Edmonds

Pause and Reflect

You can make a difference by doing simple things. Smile at a stranger you pass today. Put some quarters in someone's parking meter. Ask an elderly person if you can help carry his groceries to the car. Remember: your life is your message.

LIFE LESSON #3:
USE ALL YOUR LIFELINES

Everyone needs help from everyone.

BERTOLT BRECHT

The popular television quiz show *Who Wants to Be a Millionaire?* allows contestants to use "lifelines" if they need help answering a question. They can ask the audience for help. They can ask the computer for help. Or they can phone a friend for the answer, one of five prearranged people they've selected with as wide a variety of knowledge as possible: a movie buff, a scientist, a university professor, for example. It's a fun show. The only moments worse than a contestant's failure to answer correctly are the ones where she answers incorrectly *without having used all her lifelines!*

What lifeline do you reach for when you don't know the answer? How do you deal with fear, or worry, or life's big decisions? Have you ever even considered what lifelines are available to you? And are you using all of them?

Lifelines are the things you can't live without, the things that feed you, body and spirit. They include walking, meditation, the gym, writing, dancing, quilting, walleyball, swimming with dolphins, volunteering, a good book, your doctor, your pastor, your faith, and family. Ellen goes to the gym three times a week; Sue does yoga every day. At eighty-three, my mother finds her lifeline on the tennis courts.

Al-Anon is one of my most important lifelines, as is meditation. But, like *Millionaire,* my number one lifeline is my "phone-a-friend" list.

I used to try to be friends with everyone I met: the beautiful young woman at the cosmetics counter in Salt Lake City, the concert organizer in New York, my yoga teacher's teenaged son. Let's face it: I like people! But over time I found that I was depleting myself in an effort to maintain friendships with so many people—even if it was just through a card at Christmas. I now count six women and one man in my circle of closest friends. In case of emergency—mental, physical, or spiritual—I would not hesitate to call any one of them in the middle of the night.

But what can you do if you feel you have no one to call in the middle of the night? Think bigger. Wider. Unconventionally. Think government and social service agencies. Think people just waiting to help you. We have free clinics and libraries and civil liberties unions and lawyers' associations that might offer to take your case *pro bono* (for free). We have support groups of every kind imaginable. We have 12-Step programs to help you in your fight against alcoholism, overeating, gambling, debt, sex addiction, and many others. We have counselors and ministers we can turn to. And the worldwide web to tell us how to find anything, anywhere, any time.

If you don't have a computer or don't do well with the Internet, put the number of your local library on your refrigerator. It's filled with extraordinary reference librarians who know how to help you find anything you need—and who will do so happily.

The point is this: reach out. Ask for help. That's what Paul Dunion did when his daughter Sarah was born. He didn't really have a choice. Nevertheless, he soon learned the truth of Maya Angelou's words in her poem "Alone": "Nobody, but nobody/Can make it out here alone."

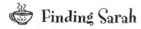 Finding Sarah

In March of 1975 a child arrived into my life who filled my heart with joy, but whose presence would shatter my paternal dreams and idyllic visions of family life. By the arrival of her first birthday, my daughter Sarah was diagnosed with severe mental retardation and cerebral palsy. The cerebral palsy would mean some form of physical disability; the mental retardation put her IQ at about 40—about the same as my golden retriever. With her diagnosis came my new identity as Sarah's victim.

As a teenager I had been somewhat of a Golden Boy,

accustomed to success and popularity. My heroic attitude perpetuated throughout early adulthood, characterized by a confidence that I would certainly enjoy the favor of the gods. Sarah's disability fractured my faith in the justice of life.

The task of caring for her was daunting. However, I refused to completely let go of my heroic grip on life and began to direct my valiant efforts toward supporting Sarah. Her mother and I took on the stewardship of Sarah's development as our personal mission. She required twenty-four-hour care, because her little body was prone to sudden unpredictable movements that could endanger her. Our marriage, our family, and our life were about work.

By age two Sarah was undergoing occupational and physical therapy regularly. I was deeply committed to her walking. I filled a little plastic shopping cart—like the ones in the supermarket—with weights so she could lean on it. We practiced with it every day, and within seven months she was walking and we were making the rounds of the neighborhood every afternoon.

Milestones like this always gave us hope for the next big accomplishment. But by her third birthday the injurious impact of her disability upon her physical and intellectual development was glaring. Refusing to succumb to a haunting sense of hopelessness, we began to research alternative approaches to Sarah's condition, and soon found a neurological rehabilitation program that we thought had the potential to impact Sarah's development.

"Patterning," as it was called, consisted of a series of exercises and movements aimed at stimulating lower brain activity. The only problem was that the program had to be done in one-hour intervals, seven hours per day, six days per week. We calculated that we would need 100 volunteers, with two people working with Sarah every hour.

We were incredibly naïve, but our love for Sarah was strong. Without grasping the enormity of the task, we put an ad in the paper asking for volunteers, and invited people to a meeting where they could meet Sarah and hear what we needed. We got our volunteers—about 60 percent from the community and 40 percent from the students at the college where I was teaching. And thus a patterning program began in the Dunion home and continued for three years. It was the first time in my life that I had ever asked for help.

Our home resembled a community center with a constant stream of people moving in and out. Our son spent more time at the neighbor's than at home, while our daughter Jenny sat on the outside step of the house, telling the volunteers to go away.

As the months passed, it was extremely difficult to measure any improvement in Sarah's symptoms. But it would have been impossible to miss the joy Sarah took in being with so many caring people.

After three years, however, we left the patterning

experience behind us. It was taking its toll on our two able-bodied children, and our marriage was under a lot of strain. The only option we had was to enroll Sarah in the special needs program in the local school system. She stayed in this program into high school, and from six to sixteen, mostly "maintained." She was quiet, pretty, still out of control of her body, and prone to "episodes." I could turn my back for a second in the grocery store, then turn around to an entire shelf being wiped out. We knew Sarah couldn't communicate, and we thought a lot of her behavior was just acting out.

Yet one thing caught our attention periodically. From time to time a specialist would visit the school to consult with the special needs program. On three separate occasions we had notes from the school telling us of the consultant's opinion that something about Sarah was unusual. They'd say things like, "I've been around severe mental retardation for twenty-five years, and there's something odd here. There's something about her eye contact that doesn't fit the script." But nobody could tell us what it was.

From time to time, we advertised at the local colleges and universities for students to do some daytime care for her, which would free us up for a few hours. One day a young woman took the job, and within two weeks we noticed some strange and remarkable things. Normally, we could not take Sarah out in public, for example to a restaurant, because she would wipe out everything on the table within ninety seconds. Even at home, when we brought in certain people to work with her, chaos would break out.

But if Christine was with her, Sarah would be perfectly calm. Christine had no expertise—she was just a college student going to school—but there was some emotional connection between the two that gave Sarah more security, confidence, and control.

Shortly before Sarah's sixteenth birthday, a speech therapist from the local university contacted us and told us he had just learned about an innovative communication technique at a conference he'd attended, one that might serve Sarah. It meant someone having to work with Sarah, and Christine readily agreed to go to his office with Sarah to give it a try. The technique used a keyboard and, immediately following the meeting, we got a call from the therapist telling us, "Your daughter just spelled out that her father's name is Paul, and her mother's name is Amy."

I didn't believe it.

Shortly thereafter, we were contacted by Sarah's principal requesting an emergency meeting in order to evaluate Sarah's educational goals.

Sarah's mother and I had grown somewhat calloused by the bureaucracy that had besieged us through the years and thought this was just a case of the administrator tightening some loose ends in Sarah's special needs program. When we arrived at the meeting we were surprised not to see the usual half-dozen therapists and teachers but rather a room filled with some two-dozen educators.

The principal began by saying, "Mr. and Mrs. Dunion, I'm going to get right to the point. Your daughter Sarah hung a banner in the cafeteria yesterday that read, 'I'm Sarah Dunion, I'm intelligent and I deserve your respect.'"

After the initial shock, we heard report after report explaining how the new communication technique being used by Sarah was revealing a minimum of average intelligence with above-average verbal aptitude.

Her diagnosis was changed from mental retardation and cerebral palsy to pachygyria, a rare disease affecting only 600 people in the world. Sarah is one of only three people in the world known to have her specific version of the disease.

Sarah went on to graduate from high school. At age nineteen she asked to have her own place. One of the people in the support circle we belong to worked for an agency that was able to help her turn that dream into a reality. At twenty-eight, Sarah bought her own house! She still needs twenty-four-hour care because she is still not in control of her body, but she has live-in help. She interviews and hires her own staff. She continues to make progress, and she just recently began typing with two hands instead of one. She has even been able to fill us in on some of her experiences of earlier life. It turns out she was never acting out, as we had thought, but simply unable to control her body.

Sarah is now thirty-two, a writer, and, with the help of a computerized voice, lecturer and consultant to social service agencies and families who have a member with a disability. She has even lectured in London.

Sarah has been a teacher whom I would not have consciously welcomed into my life—and one I cannot afford to lose. Through her, I learned to loosen my grip on my need to be heroic and in doing so, found enough strength to ask for help. I learned that Sarah was a mirror of the most vulnerable and fragile parts of myself. I was never really Sarah's victim but my own, as I maintained an adversarial relationship with my own vulnerability. I mostly learned that life is about being willing to face everything that happens to us, learning which limits can be overcome and which ones we must learn to make peace with. Ultimately, in finding Sarah, I learned how to find myself.

Paul Dunion

Pause and Reflect

1. Where do you feel stuck right now? Commit yourself to finding a resource that can help you. It might be a person, a book, an organization, a group, a friend, a magazine, a counselor, a minister, a helpline—be creative.
2. Make a list of Personal Help Resources for you to call on in times of need.

LIFE LESSON #4:
LEARN HOW TO LISTEN

*Nature has given to men one tongue, but two
ears, that we may hear from others twice as
much as we speak.*

EPICTETUS

All humans are very much alike, it turns out. While ongoing research constantly reveals more on the subject, estimates on the genetic similarities among human beings have gone as high as 99.9 percent.[1]

Is it possible that less than 1 percent of our biological makeup can really account for the vast differences we humans display? Beyond the obvious physical differences, what about the myriad cultural, religious, political, and philosophical beliefs that either draw us together or pull us apart? We seem to be so different from so many others, but are we really? Don't we human beings, in general, aspire to the same things?

This question was answered for me one day on a flight, when I found myself sitting next to an emergency medical technician (EMT) in the Army National Guard. He was returning from eighteen months of service in Iraq.

The experience had had a profound impact on him. Stationed in Kurdistan, he had connected deeply with the people, whom he described as happy, even among the poorest. When I asked him how he had connected with the Kurds, he said, "It all comes down to listening. The Kurds love to sing and tell stories. Whenever possible, I would take off my weapon, remove the gear, and sit with them. Despite my level of activity, I always tried to stop and just listen to them."

He observed that people are the same everywhere—that these people had the same needs and hopes as most: to be treated decently, to have their kids go to school, and to live in a world free from fear.

Listening, I thought, *the secret weapon.*

If you want to see whether you're a good listener, notice whether you let people finish their sentences. The tendency to interrupt others means your listening skills could use improvement. But it's worth it. We all know how to talk, but when we learn how to listen, we become skilled in the other half of true communication.

In the next story, Leah Green shows us the profound depth of human experience that occurs when we allow ourselves to listen to and receive from one another. She shows us that when we listen fully, we can discover common ground—even with our enemies.

☕ The Secret Weapon

It was 1991. The first Intifada, the Palestinian uprising against the Israelis, was raging. A group of Americans and I walked quietly through the twisted alleys of the Al-Fawwar refugee camp near Hebron. We could hear Israeli soldiers moving through the other side of the camp. We turned a corner and came upon a middle-aged Palestinian woman picking through rubble. Our host explained to her that we had come to listen to the people of Israel and Palestine—to see the situation firsthand and listen to their stories.

The woman turned to us and, gesturing at the pile of rubble with despair, began to speak. "This was my home," our host translated. The woman cried with rage as she told us that her youngest son had been shot and killed by the Israeli Army, and her oldest son had just been sentenced to life in prison by a military court. After the sentence had been handed down, her home had been bulldozed. She and her two daughters were left with only the makeshift shed that housed their animals. The woman began to wail, and our host translated: "Why do Americans hate us? What have we done to you? We've lost everything! We are just struggling to survive." We stood in shock as she continued to give voice to her anger and her grief. For most in the group, this was their first awareness that many Palestinians believed the United States was waging war on them.

Then we saw the real power of listening, when, having vented her fury, she took out a handkerchief, wiped her eyes, and invited us inside her shed for tea. We sat with her on her dirt floor, drank watered-down sweet tea, and began a memorable exchange, listening openly and respectfully to one another.

I had been involved in Israeli-Palestinian reconciliation since 1982 when, as a young woman, I participated in a training at the School for Peace in Israel. The Israelis and Palestinians came together, often for the first time in their lives, to connect with one another as human beings. I saw that when people shared the simple truth of their own stories and their own personal suffering, their adversaries could listen without blame and without debate. A bond was formed between them, and a small space of peace was created.

In 1990 I began experimenting with another approach: I started taking Americans to the Middle East to listen to the stories of Israelis and Palestinians. I felt it would be healing for those in the conflict and enlightening for the Americans. After many successful listening trips to the Middle East, we become known as The Compassionate Listening Project, whose goal was to build international support for peace in the Middle East, while offering a practical tool for conflict resolution among the people "on the ground" in those countries.

The fundamental premise of Compassionate Listening is

that every party to a conflict is suffering, and every act of violence comes from an unhealed wound. Our job as peacemakers is to hear the grievances of all parties and find ways to tell each side about the humanity and the suffering of the other. Americans who participate in the project are trained to listen respectfully to all sides.

In 1998 we began teaching Compassionate Listening workshops to Israelis and Palestinians so they could continue the work themselves in their communities. One of our first workshops included Ester, an Israeli Holocaust survivor in her late seventies, and Mary, a Christian Palestinian in her early twenties. For both of them, this was their first time coming face to face to listen to the personal suffering of their adversaries.

On the second day, twenty-five of us formed a circle to listen to Ester and Mary tell their stories. Ester went first and started by telling us how she had grown up in Germany and been sent to England during World War II when she was fifteen years old. Her brother and sister had also escaped, but her parents had been killed in Auschwitz. Ester eventually married and moved to Palestine, which would soon become Israel.

Ester told us what it was like raising a family in the new state of Israel and living through so many wars—how heartbroken she was that Jewish families could not live without the threat of violence, after all the persecution and terror they had lived through in Europe. She talked about how sad it was for her that her children and grandchildren have all been in the army and suffered terrible effects from the war and the fighting. She described living with the constant fear of suicide bombers and her daily concern for her family and friends.

While Ester spoke, Mary, the young Palestinian woman, who had never had personal contact with an Israeli Jew before, sat and listened to her story and cried just like the rest of us. Mary acknowledged Ester's pain, and her heart opened to an Israeli Jew for the first time in her life.

Then it was Mary's turn. She sat quietly and told us what it was like to grow up under Israeli military occupation in Jerusalem. She told us about schoolmates she had lost. One schoolmate was riding home from school on a bicycle and was shot in the back by an Israeli soldier. He fell off his bike and died right in front of her and her classmates.

She told us about another time when she was surrounded and harassed by Israeli soldiers on her way home from school. She was terrified that she was going to be dragged away and killed, and that her family would never know what had happened to her. Her story was one of day-to-day harassment and humiliation. She trembled the whole time she was telling her story. By the end, her body was shaking violently.

When Mary finished, the group wiped their eyes and sat in silence, taking in these two incredibly painful stories.

Then Ester got up, walked across the room and embraced Mary as if she were her own granddaughter. Mary cried in her arms, and Ester rocked her and comforted her. We all shed tears yet again, overwhelmed to be witnessing the first loving, human contact between these former enemies.

Over the following years, Ester maintained contact with Mary. They had bonded during the workshop and made a connection that has lasted to this day, despite the ongoing conflict. One year Ester even brought her friends from Germany to meet Mary at her workplace, a beautiful convent in the old city of Jerusalem. Here was a Jewish woman bringing her German friends to meet her Palestinian friend! When I saw Ester not long ago, she told me, "You should have seen the sparkle in Mary's eyes when I walked in the door that first time!"

Once people have humanizing contact with one person from the other side, anything and everything becomes possible. The stage has been set for those two individuals to be able to envision peace. And I think this is the most important thing. Even if a peace agreement is made at the political level, it will take people on the ground like Mary and Ester to build real peace between people.

Once a heart opens to the other side, it can never completely shut again. This is how I believe real change occurs—one person, one heart, at a time.

Leah Green

Pause and Reflect

1. What's your stronger communicating skill: speaking or listening? Consider for a moment that listening is just as important a skill as speaking. Is it possible that your potential to listen to others is a strength you didn't know you had?

2. The next time you talk with someone (really, whether it's your boss, your partner, your child, someone calling on the phone), try listening without interrupting. If you feel any "charge" arising in you, ask them if you can get back to them later after you've had time to reflect on the matter. Then be sure to follow up, once you've had a chance to get clear about your response and you're sure there's no charge left.

Life Lesson #5:
Be Open to Possibility

In the dark time, the eye begins to see.

Theodore Roethke

Soon after graduating from college in Baton Rouge, I moved to Washington, D.C. I wanted to experience life in a big city, and our nation's capital seemed liked a perfect match for my journalism skills and political interests.

On my own for the first time, I loved living in a place where the national and local news were the same. Every day I walked from my Dupont Circle apartment downtown to various temporary secretarial and office jobs. I was a "Kelly Girl," as they were called in those days, and the great thing about being a Kelly Girl in Washington was that I had jobs like a three-month stint with a presidential commission. I also fell in love, and my boyfriend and I were so compatible that we never had an argument. Life was grand!

One day while walking to work, the thought passed through my mind: there's got to be something more to life. I didn't think much of it, but the thought began to reoccur every morning as I walked past beautifully landscaped homes and impressive government buildings.

Then one morning, passing the Peace Corps building on my usual route, something made me stop. I stood outside the building for a moment, asking myself what I was doing, then walked in. I asked for an application, filled it out over the next couple of weeks, then dropped it off one morning on my way to work.

A couple of months later, I was accepted. My mind couldn't make sense of it. Was I really going to leave this wonderful, rich life to go to Africa for two years? I felt as if I was standing on the edge of a precipice, wondering whether to jump.

I jumped. I couldn't help myself. Although I didn't understand what was happening at the time, the impulse to expand my life beyond "the box" could not be denied. I left my boyfriend, my family, and my friends—not to mention electricity and hot running water—for an adventure into the unknown. I was terrified, but nothing could stop the quiet joy I felt inside at the possibilities that compelled me forward to a new life.

The story you are about to read confirms my belief that when we stay open to possibility, we open a space in our lives to draw the people, places, and things we need to fulfill our desires and our purpose.

One final note: a couple of years ago, my mother handed me a shoe box containing every letter and postcard I had written home during my three years in the Peace Corps and traveling around the world. There were about 125 all together. "I thought it possible that you might want to write a book some day," she said.

☕ Well of Strength

A large portion of Senegal is covered by the massive, encroaching Sahel Desert, which is harsh and unfriendly—even to the plants and animals that typically inhabit deserts. The pale orange sand is fine, like dust, and is so pervasive that everything near the desert's edge is covered with it: the streets, houses, plants, roads—and the people.

We were there, eighteen Hunger Project contributors and leaders, to help the people of a desert village find a new source of water, or a new place to live. As our drivers took the vehicles deep into the desert, we became covered with fine silty sand. It burrowed into our lungs with every breath. We saw fewer and fewer people, plants and animals, and soon there was nothing but barren land. It was hot and dry, over 95 degrees Fahrenheit. It seemed unimaginable that any human being could live in this climate.

Our Senegalese drivers knew the desert well. When our rough, unpaved road disappeared into the sand, they began driving on the open desert by compass only. At one point the front vehicle stopped and the driver turned off his engine. The other two followed suit. After listening awhile, we heard the faint sound of drums. Our driver smiled, turned on his engine, and began driving toward its source. As we drove, the rhythm grew louder, and soon we could see tiny specks moving on the horizon. Initially, we thought the specks were animals but soon realized they were children, dozens of children running toward our vehicles, bursting with excitement.

Beyond them we noticed two large baobab trees standing alone in the desolate vastness. The baobab is a lifesaving tree that can grow with almost no water and provides shade and a windbreak for desert dwellers.

Under the trees, about 120 people gathered in the precious shade. There were drummers in the center of an opening in the crowd, and inside the circle women danced. As the distance between us closed, the drumming filled the air with a vibrant energy, and the celebration grew more intense. We picked up some of the children in our cars and others ran alongside.

The incredible scene seemed to have risen out of nothing—men, women, and children—dancing, drumming, cheering, clapping, and shouting greetings of welcome to our small visiting delegation. We climbed out of our vehicles, and dozens of women ran to us, dressed in beautiful traditional Senegalese headdresses and long cotton *boubous*— loose, colorful dresses. It was a welcome like no other.

They seemed to know I was the leader, and they pulled me into the center of the circle, where they danced around me and with me. I was swept up in the moment, moving my body in concert with theirs in a freeing, natural rhythm. My fellow travelers joined me, and we danced and clapped and laughed together. Time and space seemed suspended. It wasn't hot or dry anymore. It wasn't sandy or windy. All that disappeared, and we were enveloped in celebration. We were one.

The drums suddenly stopped. It was time for the meeting to begin. People sat down on the sand and the chief identified himself. With the help of our translator, he explained that their village was several kilometers away and that they had come to welcome us and were grateful for our offer of partnership. He said they were a strong and able tribe and that the desert was their spiritual home—the only home they had ever known. But they and sixteen other villages to the east were at a point where scarce water resources were pushing them to the edge of their options.

Government services were not extended to these people, even in times of crisis. They were illiterate, could not vote, and went uncounted in the census. The tribe had tremendous resilience, but their shallow wells were nearly dry, and to see themselves through this next dry season, they needed new thinking—fast.

They were Muslim, and as we sat together in a circle to discuss the situation, the men did all the talking. The women sat in a second circle where they could hear and see, but not speak. I could feel the women's power behind me and sensed that they would be key in the solution. In this barren orange land, a solution seemed impossible, but the group's dignity and resilience argued differently. There was a way through, and together we would find it.

I asked to meet only with the women. It was a strange request in this Muslim culture, where the *mullahs* and chief were empowered to speak for all, but they allowed it. The women from my team gathered with the tribal women on the hot ground and drew in close. Our translator was a man, and the *mullahs* allowed him to join us.

Several tribal women spoke immediately, saying there was an underground lake beneath the area. They could feel it; they had seen it in visions. All they needed was our help to get permission from the men to dig a well deep enough to reach the water. The men had refused; they did not believe the water was there and didn't want the women to do that kind of work.

The women spoke with convincing strength, and I felt a rush of collective energy and commitment. I looked around me. It was baking hot. There were thousands of flies. I had silt in my mouth and lungs. It was about as uncomfortable a place as you can imagine, and yet I did not feel any thirst or discomfort—only the presence of possibility amidst these bold, beautiful women.

When we set out into the Sahel Desert, I'd feared we would encounter people who were hopeless, starving, sick, and poor. These people definitely needed more food and water, but they were not "poor." They were eager to create a way through this challenge, and they burned with the fire of possibility. They were a well of strength, perseverance, and ingenuity. They wanted our partnership—not hand-outs, money, or food—and respect and equal partnership is what we brought.

After many conversations with both the women and men, the *mullahs* and chief agreed to allow the women to begin digging the well. Over the next year, as the community rationed its existing supplies of water, the women dug both with hand tools and the simple equipment we brought them. They dug deeper and deeper into the ground, singing, drumming, and caring for each other's children as they worked, never doubting that the water was there.

The men watched skeptically but allowed the work to continue. The women, however, were anything but doubt-ful. They were certain that if they dug deep enough, the water would be there. And it was! They reached the under-ground lake of their visions.

In the years since, the tribe has built a pumping system and a water tower for storage. Not just one, but seventeen villages now have water. The whole region is transformed and flourishing. Women's leadership groups in all seventeen villages are the centers of action. There is irrigation and chicken farming. There are literacy classes and batiking businesses. People are flourishing, and they are contributing members of their country. They face new challenges and meet them with the same dignity and commitment.

The women are now a respected part of the community in a new way, with greater access to leadership, and the tribe is proud that it was their own people, their own work, and the land they lived on that proved to be the key to their own prosperity.

Lynne Twist

Pause and Reflect

1. What does intuition feel like to you? Is it a thought or a sensation in your body?
2. Are you facing a tough decision now? What is the small voice inside you telling you about it? Does one choice make you feel comfortable and at ease in your body? Does the other make you contract? Pay attention to your body's wisdom.

TO THINE OWN SELF BE TRUE

And you? When will you begin
that long journey into yourself?

Rumi

Life Lesson #1:
Tell the Truth

You will never find yourself
until you face the truth.

Pearl Bailey

Could Shakespeare have known that lines spoken by his characters would endure for centuries? What better language could express one of the most important ideas for personal transformation in our time than these famous words from *Hamlet:* "This above all: to thine ownself be true." What did Shakespeare really mean by that? And how many of us stop to absorb what follows that line: "And it must follow, as the night the day, Thou canst not then be false to any man"? In other words, we can't really be true to anyone else unless we're first true to ourselves.

Usually it's the opposite in our culture. Care giving is natural to women—in fact, we've mastered it. We look after partners, children, friends, employees, coworkers, clients and pets—and now, many of us are facing the significant task of caring for aging parents. It's no surprise, then, that one of the biggest issues facing women today is how to find time for ourselves.

What is surprising, however, is that we have been so cultured to put the needs of others first, that many of us don't have a clue how to take care of ourselves. In fact, we're taught that it's selfish to do so!

But making others the center of our lives can have devastating effects on a woman's health and well-being. As Dr. Joyce Brothers says, "The most important advice I can give a woman when it comes to juggling career and marriage is to put herself first. Selfish? Not at all. After all, whose life is it?"[1]

"*What?*" you say. The first time this idea was put forth on *Oprah,* by guest life-coach and author Cheryl Richardson, the audience booed. Oprah doesn't allow booing on her show, and she attempted damage control by pointing out that it's the oxygen mask theory: Put your mask on first, before tending to children or helping others.[2]

Putting ourselves last on the to-do list, says Joan Borysenko in *A Woman's Journey to God,* is one of the hardest things about being a woman in a busy world. "While both genders can fall into the doing trap, women have a harder time getting out. . . . The big question becomes, 'How can I get what I need without being selfish to others?' As long as we think that spending time on ourselves is selfish, the vicious jaws of the doing trap will stay locked around our ankles."

Elinor Hall had been married more than thirty years when she realized she didn't fully know who she was. The story that follows is the poignant and powerful telling of how she discovered what being true to yourself really means.

☕ A New Truth

I had to get away. I was in my car driving through some of the most breathtaking scenery in the Southwest, and I barely saw it. I knew the road to Zion National Park, but it wasn't the towering canyon walls and the multifaceted sandstone rocks that captured my attention as they usually did. The question "Who are you?" was ringing in my ears, causing my stomach to clench and my eyes to see only the road I knew so well.

During my thirty-two years of marriage, I had never gone off on my own to spend time with just myself. There had been visits with my family and spiritual retreats, but never time on my own without a stated and long-planned purpose. And here I was on my way to check into a motel to try to find the answer to that question.

A few days before, I had been participating in a personal growth seminar and, in the course of a discussion on truth, the course leader asked me: "Who are you?" I stumbled around a bit and mumbled a few words like "loving," "kind," and "compassionate," but I knew I was only touching the surface. I even mentioned the word "power," but quickly dismissed it as I began sobbing.

I had been afraid of that question all my life. I had actually disdained the practice of looking deeply inside and examining all facets of one's life in an attempt at self-knowledge. I thought it was self-centered and, from my friends' accounts of their experiences, quite painful. Why would I want to do that?

Now, I not only *wanted* to do that, I knew I *had* to. And so I chose to go to a place that has always nurtured my soul and soothed my busy mind.

After I got settled into my motel room, tucked at the base of the rocks, I went into the park and found my way to the Virgin River. It was early spring, with a clear blue sky and gentle breeze. I sat on the banks of the river in the warm sun and began to write in my journal.

Everything was up for examination and review, and I began with what I thought was the easiest part of my life to look at: my job. I had the perfect job, in the perfect location, working with the perfect people. Why didn't it always feel like that? Why did I often feel frazzled and unsure? Who was I trying to impress?

I had always been a "pleaser"—followed the rules, always said yes to requests for help, offered my time, my energy and often my heart without much, if any, thought about what was good for me, what nurtured me. In fact, I had no idea that I should even consider nurturing myself.

The need to please was as real to me as the need to eat or sleep or love.

I continued to write. I moved with the sun in order to stay warm and kept moving through my life in my journal. When I looked at my marriage, I saw that my need to please and take care of another was pivotal. I had thought it was my "job" to ensure my husband's happiness, so I cooked only the foods that he liked; supported many "ground-floor" money-making opportunities without even thinking about their viability; did whatever it took to maintain peace, including and most especially not speaking out my true feelings if there was any sign of discomfort—his or mine.

Whenever anyone asked me what the secret of our long marriage was I would always respond that it was kindness. As I looked at the bottom line of our marriage, that day by the river, I saw that kindness can take many forms. I realized there is no kindness to myself or my partner if I am not free to speak my truth.

My relationship with money was next. Finances had always been a struggle during my marriage. We had no children and I worked throughout our marriage, and yet it seemed that often we barely had enough. We had been through two bankruptcies pursuing my husband's dreams of making a significant contribution to the world, and here we were again with mounting debt and no concrete plans for the newest business venture. I experienced a deep level of anger, something I rarely allowed myself to feel or acknowledge—anger at my husband and his style of functioning, but most especially anger at myself for "stuffing and swallowing." I knew that I could not live like this any longer. My heart and soul would not allow it. We needed a major financial overhaul and some gentle reconnecting from a place of mutual respect. Was it possible? I had no idea.

As the sun set, I returned to my hotel and continued writing. I put together a budget and came up with some "financial rules to consider." Exhausted, I fell into bed and slept through the night.

The next day, after breakfast, I went to the east end of Zion, where there are very few marked trails and not many visitors. I scrambled over rocks in familiar places and explored new places. Energy coursed through my body. I felt free, almost giddy at times. I didn't think about what I had written the day before and did not think about what would happen when I returned home. I was filled with the power and the beauty of the place and sensed that the power I had been so afraid to even consider was right there in me.

When I returned home at the end of the day, I had no plan for what to do next. After a couple of days I asked Ron if he would like to know about my time at Zion. I shared my writings with him—and kept going even though the discomfort was high. When I finished, it was Ron who tearfully asked if I thought we should separate. When I replied that I didn't know, and asked him what he thought, he said: "It looks that way."

It took us six months to feel our way into separation and another year before I walked into the District Court—intentionally alone—and filed the divorce papers. During that time, we spoke more openly and honestly than we ever had. The pain was sometimes almost unbearable, but we both came to the realization that we didn't have the energy or the desire to go through the major changes that were required to rebuild the marriage.

Today, that power I glimpsed two years ago in the park continues to show itself in big and small ways. Ron and I are friends, forging a new relationship based on acceptance and respect. I love my new life—for the first time ever I am buying coffee ice cream and balancing my checkbook. I bought my first car solo. I have an attorney and an accountant. I have moved into a place of leadership in my work. I am free to create my life based on the simple truths of who I am, and I have come to accept those new truths with self-respect and self-love.

Elinor Daily Hall

Pause and Reflect

1. Make a list of the things you value, what's important to you. Ask yourself if these values are in abundant evidence in your life.
2. What aspects of your life are not truthful to your values? Are you staying in a bad relationship because you don't want to admit failure? Have you taken on too much? Are you not paying attention to signs from your body that you're tired and need to rest? Is it hard to get up in the morning because you don't like your job?
3. What have you been asked to do that you know you don't have time for? Try saying no, and commit to doing so without feeling guilty afterward.

LIFE LESSON #2:
DO THE RIGHT THING

There are victories of the soul and spirit.
Sometimes, even if you lose, you win.

ELIE WIESEL

Integrity is what happens when your inner voice and values line up with your words and actions. It means doing the right thing because it's the right thing to do.

I found a wonderful example of this when I came across a *Life* magazine from 1995 and opened to an article about the NBA basketball player, Hakeem Olajuwon. When he developed his namesake shoe with Spaulding, he insisted it be sold for no more than $35. He felt that $120 was too much for a working mother with three boys to pay for a pair of athletic shoes.[1] That's integrity: being so clear about your values that you make sure everything in your life lines up with them—even if it means giving up financial gain or prestige.

The *Flower Essence Repertory,* a book that describes the healing properties of flowers, says that "Consciousness must also include conscience; as the soul gains greater awareness of itself, it also acquires an inner voice or moral life. This morality must be generated from within; as long as laws or dictates are stamped on the personality from the outside, the

Self will not develop real strength of character."[2]

I recently had a chance to put my own integrity to the test. It was a small thing—but I've found that the small things are proving grounds for the big things. I had searched high and low for a local Avon representative from whom I could buy a couple of tubes of mascara that I loved. I finally found her, drove all the way to the next town to pick them up, and left her a check for $8.24.

Months later, my bank statements were still showing she'd never cashed the check. I called her. She couldn't find it and in a later phone message, told me to do whatever I felt was right. I could not in good conscience not send her the money again, so I dug through records to find her address and sent her another check. I hated spending so much time on what seemed like a relatively small amount of money.

But some time later I had another message from her on my machine. She was almost in tears as she thanked me for sending the check. The depth of her gratitude vanquished any self-judgment about how much time and energy I had spent correcting the mishap, which hadn't seemed equal to two tubes of mascara.

Linda Chaé's mark on the world of business has integrity at its core. I met Linda through a mutual friend who introduced me to skincare products developed by Linda. Her products feed my body and skin, so I feel very lucky to have discovered her for obvious personal reasons. But her story feeds my spirit and encourages me to listen more deeply to the voice of my conscience.

☕ The Beautiful Truth

At the age of twenty I was managing a beauty-care products company. When Kathy, the owner, decided to sell the business, I acquired a loan and became the proud owner of my own make-up and skin-care line. Then I found a job at a beauty salon where I could do makeup and facials with my own line. I was thrilled. Kathy had told me how natural the products were. Everything was named after fruits and vegetables. My favorite was Peach Day Cream.

I got married that same year. My mother-in-law, Julia, had breast cancer, and every night I massaged her, relieving the swelling in her arm. But as I lavished her with my Peach Day Cream, I noticed that she'd get a hard lump, sometimes two, on her chest and arm.

One day I ran out of Peach Day Cream, so I massaged Julia with some oil. The lumps disappeared.

We began to experiment with different creams, and for months I didn't use Peach Day Cream. Then one night I tried it again, only to find that within an hour Julia had two painful lumps that lasted three days.

We told the doctor what had happened. "There's no way a cream could do that," he said, irritated. He told me to stop massaging her.

Julia begged me to continue the massages, but I avoided using Peach Day Cream because I knew there must be something wrong with it.

I contacted the manufacturer and asked, "What ingredient could cause lymphatic fluid to harden?" The chemist refused to tell me the ingredients. I called back many times, and finally he provided a partial list of ingredients. Much to my surprise, there weren't any peaches in my Peach Day Cream.

I had to know more and started taking night courses in chemistry. In one course, I studied the material-safety data sheets used by manufacturers to protect their workers. For a class assignment, I ordered data sheets for the ingredients in Peach Day Cream.

A few weeks later, I learned with horror that Peach Day Cream contained six ingredients that were potentially carcinogenic.

I called the chemist. "I can't believe this," I almost screamed. "You told me these products were safe!"

"You don't understand," he said in a condescending tone. "Those are only trace amounts. The data sheet assumes the ingredient is full strength. If the powder is at full strength and gets airborne, it will create lung cancer.

But no one's breathing in your Peach Day Cream."

I argued, but he had an answer for everything. Finally he said, "You won't find any cosmetics without these ingredients. You can't hold your cream together or preserve it without them. Your product is no different from any of the others, and none of the manufacturers is worried about cancer."

For the next three weeks my Peach Day Cream sat on the shelves collecting dust. Realizing that the same ingredients were probably in the whole product line, I stopped selling everything. What should I do? Could the whole cosmetics industry be selling carcinogenic products?

A few weeks later, Edna, one of my favorite clients, who had cancer, came into my shop in a wheelchair. "Honey," she said, "I want some products. The doctor says I only have two months. And will you promise to come to my funeral and do my makeup? Don't let my friends see me ugly at my funeral."

I tried not to cry. "Of course I will, Edna."

"I want five Peach Day Creams. I love that stuff!"

I didn't know what to say. Finally, I said, "Edna, I don't think you should use Peach Day Cream. There are some ingredients that may cause cancer."

She popped up out of that wheelchair and got close to my face. "What?" she exclaimed.

I told her again.

"I wasn't so bad a year ago. I've been using this stuff for a year. Is this why I have two months to live?"

I was horrified and scared. I knew about liability and lawsuits. I found myself saying, "Now, Edna, that's when it's at full strength. These are just trace ingredients . . ." I just repeated the chemist's words.

"I don't believe one word of that and neither do you," said Edna. "I'm ashamed of you. How could you put your name on those products?"

"I'm sorry, Edna. I didn't know for sure until I got the scientific information, and I'm not selling those products any more."

Edna grabbed my hand and said, "Linda, you do something about this. I'm dying, but you're young and have the rest of your life. Make me a cream. Make every woman a cream. We deserve to look beautiful and we deserve not to die for it. You do that."

I promised her I would.

About ten weeks later I went to the funeral home and made Edna beautiful. I felt her spirit, and I knew she was in the room. I said, "Edna, I don't know if it's possible to make a safe cream, but if it is, I promise you I will do it."

After the funeral, I went to the beauty salon and swept everything off the shelves into a trash can. I went to my warehouse and bagged the rest of my inventory. Then I sat down and figured out I had just lost $32,000. I said,

"Edna, I'm never ordering them again. I'm on a mission. I'll never again sell something that could hurt anyone."

From that day on, I dedicated my life to making toxin-free beauty products. I contacted raw material suppliers, asking for healthy alternatives, begging them to find a way. And eventually they started calling me back. "Linda," they'd say, "We've got something for you . . ."

Year after year, as I worked on creating toxin-free products, the demand for natural products grew. Finally, I started my own company and created products I trusted. Women loved them! Within two weeks of an infomercial, all 25,000 items were sold. In the first year, we did $70 million in business and broke all records. *Vogue* wrote a complimentary article about me. The *Los Angeles Times* interviewed me, and I was given credit for the "go-natural" look: "Linda Chaé takes cosmetics all natural! She's our go-natural girl!"

At the age of twenty-three, thanks to Edna, I found the courage to take action for something I believed in. And thanks to Edna, I made a commitment to doing the right thing, whatever the cost. Now and then, I give her a wink and hear her saying, "Honey, you done good."

Linda Chaé

Pause and Reflect

1. Is someone pressuring you—or are you pressuring yourself—to do something that's making you feel uncomfortable? Ask yourself, *What am I feeling uncomfortable about?* What needs to happen for your response and/or actions to line up with your beliefs?

2. The next time you find yourself struggling with a decision, ask yourself which, of all the options you have to choose from, is most in line with your values.

Life Lesson #3:
Be Willing to Walk Away

Above all, be the heroine of your life, not the victim.

Nora Ephron

Have you ever invested a lot of time or money—or both—in something you later realized was not bringing the satisfaction or monetary rewards you had anticipated or hoped for?

I remember feeling scared to tell my parents that I wanted to stop taking piano lessons after eight years of study. They had made a substantial investment. They valued the arts and felt music to be an important part of my education. Worse, they had put up with my practice sessions for years! Even as a teenager I sensed consequences of walking away from something that had involved such an investment of time and money—and I felt guilty.

Sometimes it's far bigger than piano lessons. It may be a life path we've committed to. Somewhere along the way, we are suddenly startled to realize it's the wrong path, or that we've outgrown it. When we've invested time, money, education, intimacy, or belief in something or someone, it can be extremely hard to change directions.

I once had the opportunity to coauthor a book with a world-renowned psychologist. I was ecstatic when our proposal was accepted by my publisher. We talked about next steps, deadlines, publication date, etc.

But over the next couple of days, I felt uneasy. I finally admitted that after giving 100 percent of my time, effort and devotion to the book proposal for two months, I no longer wanted to do the book. My vision had changed since starting the project, and what I valued and wanted to convey was different from the original impulse and plan for the book. I had to tell both my coauthor and publisher the truth.

My willingness to walk away served us all well. My publisher agreed to go forward with the book with my coauthor if she wanted to; thus, I was a fortunate link in a potential collaboration that could serve them both. This also opened the door for me to proceed with my own book, which evolved over time into the book you are reading now.

I have known people who have changed life directions after much greater investments than two months of their time, like author Arnold Patent. Arnold gave up his twenty-five-year law practice and "the perfect life" to pursue something else, because he was honest enough to admit he was no longer happy. That takes guts. But there is no question in my mind that people like Arnold would agree with the author of this anonymous quote: "Honesty is not something to flirt with. We must be married to it."

If it no longer fits your definition of integrity, be willing to walk away.

🍵 The Faded Ribbon

The sun had just appeared over the east end of the field when the stillness was broken by the pounding hooves of galloping horses. It was going to be a perfect day for the Ox Ridge Horse Show in Darien, Connecticut.

I jumped my horse, Opportunity Knocks, back and forth over the hedge-like fence until my trainer was satisfied. "Just remember to keep a strong pace in that field and keep a steady feel of the reins." I listened closely to what Hector told me and then walked around the show grounds to let Oscar (his nickname) cool down.

I had an hour before my competition began. I gave the horse to the barn manager to groom and hurried to the equipment room. I polished my black boots and put on a tailored navy blue hunt coat. As I was pinning up my hair, my mind drifted back to the events that had brought me East.

I had started riding in the third grade, and when I was fourteen, I began to compete. At sixteen I was riding successfully on the show circuit in Minnesota, but I had reached a plateau. To fulfill my aspiration of becoming a top rider, I needed a better teacher and higher quality horse shows. I would have to leave my friends and family and take the last quarter of my junior year in high school via correspondence. Although the transition was difficult, I knew it was something I had to do.

"Where's Lane?" I heard the barn manager ask. "Her class is starting."

I came out of my daydream and threw on the black velvet hunt cap and leather gloves. The groom held Oscar as I ran into the aisle and quickly mounted.

I trotted over to the ring, wondering if all the hours of practice would pay off. When I heard the announcement on the loudspeaker, "And our next contestant is Miss Lane Hawley riding Opportunity Knocks," I entered the ring and made a warm-up circle before the first fence. Oscar was fresh and eager and we were covering the ground at a soft gallop so the fences came up right in stride. Oscar was alert to the faintest touch on the reins.

At the end of the course there was one fence far across the field. I knew that if I jumped it smoothly the class was mine. As I neared the fence I panicked. I didn't know whether to go faster or slower, but Oscar took hold of the situation and jumped the fence in perfect stride.

"Pat your horse!" Hector shouted from the rail. I knew that was his signal to the judge that he thought it was a round worthy of a top ribbon. The judging is supposed to be objective, but Hector had a lot of clout and could usually get what he wanted. I patted Oscar happily. I was elated to have had one of the best rounds of my life.

When the class was over, my number was called first

and we trotted into the ring to accept the blue ribbon. I was glowing with triumph. All my years of hard work had culminated in a win in the major leagues. However, as the day wore on the glow began to fade.

I was sitting in the bleachers when an uneasy feeling came over me. What did this ribbon really mean? Images of some of the unseemly moments I'd witnessed in the horse world began to pop up in my mind. I knew that many trainers gave their horses illegal drugs to hide their lameness. And sometimes they drugged them just to calm them down, thoroughbreds being notoriously high strung.

And that was far from the worst of it. I remembered ugly stories of backstabbing between various stables. When one barn mysteriously burned to the ground, we all believed it was arson, committed to get insurance money.

I had heard about horse sellers having vets check out a different horse than the one they were selling. I knew of horses that were bought for a few thousand dollars and then sold for $20,000. Some people hired experts to arrange fatal accidents for their magnificent grand prix show jumpers just for the insurance money.

Was this the business I wanted to devote my life to? Were these the people I wanted to spend my life with? I got up and walked around to clear my head. I had closed my eyes to all that I knew about the horse world for a long time. Why had I tolerated it?

Suddenly the truth dawned on me. I had lost the pure experience of cantering through the fields on a crisp morning, of the smell and feel of my horse, who was enjoying the trail ride as much as I was. I had gotten caught up in the competitive frenzy—the need to win.

I wandered back to the empty tack room and sat on a trunk. It was ironic. I finally had a high caliber horse, a top trainer, and enough talent to compete in the finest horse shows. If you had asked me earlier that morning what I wanted to be when I grew up, I would have said, "a professional horse trainer." But at that moment, despite everything I had worked for, I knew this wasn't the life for me. Once I saw what blue ribbons and trophies were costing me, I didn't care about them anymore.

That night I called my parents and told them I wanted to stop riding competitively and concentrate on school my senior year. They were thrilled that I would be coming home and focusing on my education.

It's been decades now since I made that life-changing decision, and not once have I regretted it. I've always been grateful to have learned so young that if you care more about the blue ribbon than the quality of your life, that ribbon turns into nothing but a few dollars' worth of fading fabric.

Lane Hawley Cole

Pause and Reflect

Have you spent a lot of time or money, or made an emotional investment in something that no longer brings joy to your heart? Reflect on what might happen if you parted company with it: a job, a friendship, a financial investment. Would walking away be a defeat—or a victory?

LIFE LESSON #4:
TELL THE TRUTH ABOUT MONEY

Don't chase money—you'll never catch it.

DEBBI FIELDS

I was once a member of the "I'll Be Happy When" club. If I could just find the perfect mate and the perfect job—and become a millionaire quickly—then I'd be totally fulfilled.

I set out to achieve these goals with a vengeance. I thought success—especially the material kind—required it. In fact, I took a seminar on success and became proficient at setting daily, weekly, monthly, five-year—even lifetime—goals.

Dutifully, I read over my list of goals twice a day, every day. I just couldn't understand why they didn't materialize immediately. And it made me unhappy, because I had also joined the ranks of the "I Want More!" club.

In our consumer-driven society, we seem to have become money-crazed. We have adopted the collective understanding that we must have more in order to be happy and secure, and that our material success is the ultimate yardstick by which to measure our value and self-worth. Anything we like, we want to own. We are seduced by millionaires sharing their secrets and promising us that we, too, can have what they have—if we just do what they do.

While wealth can give us opportunities—travel, philanthropy, or education, for example—we hear countless stories of people who have it and yet are lonely and unfulfilled to their core. It is a curious quirk of fate that life lessons related to money can be the result of having too little of it—or too much!

A case in point was what Lynne Twist learned when she met with top women executives at Microsoft some years ago. As she describes in *The Soul of Money,* their average age was thirty-six, and their average net worth was $10 million. They rarely saw their families, and for most, their lives centered on their computers. They took little time to enjoy their material possessions and experienced very little satisfaction from their money. In fact, using their wealth to buy child-care and home-care services mainly enabled them to work longer and harder. They hoped that someday their success would bring them freedom, but, by their own admission, they were not living the lives they wanted, and as a result, they were not free.[1]

Clearly, material abundance isn't the automatic ticket to freedom that many expect. More than one-third of households in the United States are wealthier than 95 percent of the world's population and 99.9 percent of all the people who have ever walked this earth.[2,3] Yet, when Mother Teresa visited our country, she said that the United States was one of the poorest nations in the world: we suffered from the poverty of loneliness.

As Nina Wise says in her book *A Big New Free Happy Unusual Life,* "Our longing for freedom cannot be satisfied by cars or houses or diamonds; by private jets or offshore bank accounts or caviar; by miniature computers or mighty weapons. Our longing for freedom can only be satisfied by recognizing that we are each sufficient as we are, and that what feeds us has nothing to do with what we buy and everything to do with an inherent vitality of soul."[4]

Well-known certified financial planner, bestselling author, and television show host Suze Orman understands deeply the connection between money and fulfillment. Thanks to her, I'm learning what real wealth is.

True Wealth

When I was very young I had already learned that the reason my parents seemed so unhappy wasn't that they didn't love each other; it was that they never had quite enough money even to pay the bills. In our house money meant tension, worry, and sorrow. When I was about thirteen my dad owned his own business, a tiny chicken shack where he sold take-out chicken, ribs, hamburgers, hot dogs, and fries. One day the oil that the chicken was fried in caught fire. In a few minutes the whole place exploded in flames. This was when my mom and I happened to arrive on the scene, and we all stood outside watching the fire burn away my dad's business.

All of a sudden my dad realized that he had left his money in the metal cash register inside the building, and I watched in disbelief as he ran back into the inferno, in the split second before anyone could stop him. He tried and tried to open the metal register, but the intense heat had already sealed the drawer shut. Knowing that every penny he had was locked in front of him, about to go up into flames, he literally picked up the scalding metal box and carried it outside. When he threw the register on the ground, the skin on his arms and chest came with it.

He had escaped the fire safely once, untouched. Then he voluntarily risked his life and was severely injured. The money was that important. That was when I learned that money is obviously more important than life itself.

From that point on, earning money, lots of money, not only became what drove me professionally, but also became my emotional priority. Money became, for me, not the means to a life rich in all kinds of ways; money became my singular goal.

Years later this kid from the South Side of Chicago was a broker with a huge investment firm. I was rich—richer than I could have imagined. And I realized that I was profoundly unhappy; the money hadn't bought or brought me happiness. So if money wasn't the key to happiness, what was? It was then that I began a quest, which has taken me deep into the meaning of life—and the meaning of money.

I don't know if I have discovered the meaning of life, but I have learned a great deal about what money can and cannot do. And it can do a lot. Your money will work for you, and you will always have enough—more than enough—when you give it energy, time, and understanding. I have come to think that money is very much like a person, and it will respond when you treat it as you would a cherished friend—never fearing it, pushing it away, pretending it doesn't exist, or turning away from its needs, never clutching it so hard that it hurts. Sometimes it's fatter, sometimes it's skinnier, sometimes it doesn't feel so good and needs special nurturing. But if you tend it like the living entity it is, then it will flourish, grow, take care of you for as long as you need it, and look after the loved ones you leave behind.

When it comes to money, freedom starts to happen when what you do, think, and say are one. You'll never be free if you say that you have more than enough, then act as if and think you don't. You'll never be free if you think you don't have enough, then act as if and say you do. You will have enough when you believe you will and take the actions to express that belief. And you'll have more than enough when you realize that you can be rich at any income because you are more than your money, you are more than your job or title, than the car you drive or the clothing you wear. Your own power and worth are not judged by what money can sell and what money can buy; true freedom cannot be bought or sold at any price. True freedom, true wealth, is that which can never be lost.

Suze Orman

Pause and Reflect

1. Write down three of your beliefs about money, Pay attention to expressions you heard as a child such as, "Money doesn't grow on trees," and "filthy rich." Ask yourself if these expressions still influence you.
2. Write a statement that describes your current financial situation. When you talk about money to others, does what you say accurately reflect the truth of your financial state?

Life Lesson #5:
Speak for Yourself

....

Authenticity and subordination are totally incompatible.

Jean Baker Miller

Eighty-five percent of first graders have high self-esteem. But by age nine, self-esteem peaks in girls, and by the time fifth grade rolls around, that figure has dropped to 20 percent. Attend a high-school graduation and you can bet that only 5 percent of the seniors have any shred of self-worth left.

What has happened to us? Why do two out of three adults in America suffer from low self-esteem? We start out strong, creative, and powerful. As children we give our opinions freely, not stopping to evaluate whether we have something of value to offer. Then, somewhere along the way, especially for girls, we're taught that it's better to be seen than heard. Self-confidence might be construed as self-importance, so we're taught to downplay our accomplishments and our abilities. We learn that others' needs are more important than ours. We learn not to make waves, and we learn to be small, secretly knowing—and fearing, as Marianne Williamson said—that we are powerful beyond measure.

Your voice is your power. When you speak out, or take a stand for yourself, or claim the gifts you have to offer, you give others permission to do the same. Authenticity flourishes. Relationships deepen. A sense of purpose guides your life with quiet but exuberant joy.

Find your voice by telling the truth, first to yourself, then others. While it's true that the truth sometimes hurts, if delivered in the right way, it will always serve. And Meryl Runion, in the next story, can definitely speak to that.

 Some Boats Need to Be Rocked

My earliest memory of being unable to speak for myself goes back to when I was four years old. I was allowed to cross the street, one block in every direction. When our neighbor found me playing across the street, he didn't believe I had permission to cross. He brought me home in "disgrace" and ranted on and on as if he were some kind of superhero who had saved me and the planet from certain destruction. No one spoke for me.

Inwardly I screamed, "One block in any direction! I'm allowed! Why aren't you telling him?" Outwardly I could only cry. I doubt my mother understood why I cried so hard. I also doubt she understood what she taught me that day. She may have thought she taught me to put my best foot forward, but she actually taught me to put a false front forward. She taught me that if someone is likely to object to what you have to say, you don't say it. She taught me that if the truth is likely to rock the boat, you stay silent, you pretend.

So that's what I did. The first half of my life was based on the theme of putting a front forward that wouldn't rock the boat, create waves, or even cause a tiny ripple. That continued until I avoided a ripple that was really an early tsunami warning.

The tsunami was my late husband Mike's cancer. The ripple I avoided was his wrath when I voiced my concerns about early indications that something was terribly wrong. I got a clue of that when I read a passage in a book telling how Harvey Peterson beat his tumor to the punch. I was shocked to realize that Harvey's symptoms sounded just like Mike's. I showed the passage to Mike, who took the book, threw it across the room and screamed, "Damn it Meryl, I don't have cancer. And don't talk to me about it again. Don't you dare say anything to my mother."

I responded in what had become my habitual way . . . if my husband was upset with me, obviously I had done something terribly wrong. If I had done something wrong, I needed to avoid doing it again. I returned to the "safer" waters of agreeing with him. I almost drowned nine months later when I lost him to untreated cancer.

After Mike died, I considered myself a victim of his denial. It took a year for me to realize I was really a volunteer who chose to put a false front forward when heartfelt, extreme honesty was the only hope we had.

It happened at my counselor's office. He interrupted himself midsentence to ask, "Why is your hand over your mouth? Whose hand is that? Who is keeping you from speaking?"

I was stunned to realize I had my OWN hand over my mouth. I had silenced *myself*. And it had always been my own hand over my mouth. Mike could never have silenced me had I not chosen to allow it.

I silenced myself because I didn't want to rock the boat. Now I realized that some boats desperately need to be rocked. If I don't speak for myself, no one else will.

I became a woman on a mission—a mission to figure out how to rock the boats that need to be rocked without capsizing or sinking.

That was over twenty years ago. I've rocked a lot of boats since then.

It didn't happen overnight. Once I realized I had lost my voice, it took years to find it again. I started small in safe environments. I started speaking up and out in the safe haven of my counselor's office. (That was harder than you might think because my habit of "making nice" was so deeply entrenched.) I started being stronger with my son. (Was it possible that that beautiful being of light was manipulating me?) I set better boundaries with my boyfriend. (He resisted and we broke up.) I began to say no to my clients more often. (Some of them didn't like it, but I sure did!)

After ten years of reclaiming my voice, I contacted a seminar company and told them I wanted to work for them (even though I had no relevant experience.) They said no. A year later I contacted them again and told them I still wanted to work for them. They said yes. Speaking up for what I wanted worked and felt really good.

In my role as a seminar leader, I began encouraging others to address issues and be their own advocates. I noticed how empowered people become when they get the right words—what I call "Power Phrases"—to address their own hot-button issues. Sometimes they actually seem taller! I adopted a simple phrase that epitomizes my approach to communication: *Say what you mean and mean what you say, but don't be mean when you say it.*

Looking back, it's possible that had I had the words and the communication skills when my husband became ill, he would still be with me today. It was one of the most treatable kinds of cancer there was. But there are no guarantees. I still may have lost him—but I would not have lost myself. It's much easier to weather losses and setbacks when you were true to yourself at every turn.

When I compare life now to my "pretsunami life," the contrast is stunning. I used to live in a constant state of resentment. Now I've almost forgotten what resentment feels like. I used to have chronically conflicted emotions. Now inner conflict is rare for me. But best of all, while I used to hide behind a false front, I'm authentic now. I love being me. And I love helping others be themselves.

I also love saying what I mean and meaning what I say without being mean when I say it.

Meryl Runion

Pause and Reflect

1. Are you in a situation at home or work where you have not spoken freely? What needs to happen in order for you to speak up and say what you really feel?

2. Has someone made a promise on your behalf without checking with you first? Try to kindly but firmly let that person know that, while you appreciate her efforts to be supportive, next time you would prefer to speak for yourself. (Then congratulate yourself for speaking up for yourself!)

3. What has been left unspoken or not communicated that you feel ashamed of, and who would be the most trusted person to share that with?

Essential Ingredient

GETTING BEYOND RIGHT AND WRONG

Nothing is either good or bad.
It's thinking that makes it so.

William Shakespeare

Life Lesson #1:
Clean Up Your Past

The weak can never forgive.
Forgiveness is the attribute of the strong.

MOHANDAS GANDHI

Many of the physical aches and pains we carry around with us have their roots in the past. It might have been a sprained ankle at age six, or a teacher's comment that you weren't pretty enough to be in the school beauty pageant. Most would prefer to leave those kinds of memories in the past, and that's fine—unless they've continued to walk with you right into your present and are adversely affecting the way you think and act today. If that's the case, then it may be time to take care of your past.

Taking care of your past usually means forgiving someone for an injustice or wrong we perceive they "did" to us. It may be easier said than done, but it's well worth it. Forgiveness has become "a hot new way" to manage anger, cut stress, and improve health.

A large and growing number of books are devoted to learning how to forgive. Many contain inspiring stories, such as the famous one of Nelson Mandela, who, after serving twenty-seven years in prison for his political beliefs, invited his prison guards to his inauguration as president of South Africa.[1]

Countless others who have been deeply wronged have reported that they could find no peace until they found forgiveness. And author Catherine Ponder says it can even be a technique for becoming rich.[2] All in all, forgiveness has such far-reaching benefits that it seems we would all want to practice it every day.

I decided to give it a try. I asked myself what needed to be forgiven from my past. Two people with whom I had invested a significant amount of money came to mind immediately. They had not paid me back as they had agreed, and I resented it. And I wasn't sure whether I *wanted* to forgive them.

But deep down I knew that forgiving someone doesn't mean that what they did was okay, or that we should let ourselves be treated unfairly. It means to stop feeling victimized and stop making others responsible for our lives. In blaming the couple with whom I had invested money, I was sidestepping my own responsibility. I had given them my money, and now I was giving them the power to determine my happiness. No wonder my back ached.

Yes, research has found that forgiveness can reduce chronic back pain, decrease stress by up to 50 percent, increase energy, and improve mood, sleep, and overall physical vitality.[3]

But for Susan Brandis Slavin, author of the next story, taking care of her past was about something deeper than relief from physical symptoms. As with all stories about forgiveness, her story illustrates the truth often attributed to Corrie ten Boom: "To forgive is to set a prisoner free and to discover the prisoner was you."

☕ My Sweet Revenge

I sometimes joke that my family would have aspired just to be dysfunctional. My father suffered from a nervous disorder that made him shake all the time, and my mother spent her time either berating my father or retreating into a fantasy world. And my younger sister's problems were severe. Dolly had been an adorable but hyperactive little girl. As she got older, she eventually became a paranoid schizophrenic. Given to violent outbursts, she was obsessed with my mother, which made me her enemy. If I even tried to be in the same room with my mother, Dolly would scream and threaten both of us. Totally overwhelmed, my parents gave in to her every whim.

I was thirteen when our family moved to Los Angeles, where my father hoped to find a better job. I was thrilled, as I had always known I wanted to be an actress. But Dolly immediately insisted that she and my mother move back to Chicago—and she got her way. That left me alone with my mentally unstable father. I was frightened, but that year I discovered the theater program at my school, and it became my lifeline. In my first year, a well-known Hollywood casting director saw me in a play and cast me as Anne in a local production of *The Diary of Anne Frank.* By the time I finished junior high, I was already "in the business" as a professional actress.

When my mother and sister returned from Chicago two years later, I hoped these achievements would win me some of my mother's attention. But she was so overwrought most of the time she hardly seemed to know I existed. The only outlet for my loneliness and sorrow was acting. This made me a "deep" actress for my age, and by the time I was in the twelfth grade, I had amassed a large collection of trophies. They were precious to me and gave me a glimmer of hope that I might be worth something.

Then one day I came home from school and found my trophies were gone. Only a few pieces of bent metal remained, scattered around the floor. *What had my sister done to them? And why had my mother let her?* I started screaming wildly as I fell to the floor and lay there sobbing. I cried until there were no more tears, and finally looked up at Dolly, standing silently beside my mother. She looked at me with a faint smile on her face, and I realized she had won. I couldn't fight her for a piece of my mother any longer. *She's yours!* I cried inside. *Who cares about any of you, anyway?*

I stood up, and for the first time in my young life, I felt the power of cold rage. I would close my heart to them and become a success. Someday I would get even. I would prove myself to the world, become famous—and never speak to them again. I would make them sorry they had not seen me for who I was.

A few months later, I graduated from high school and immediately moved to New York City. I worked fervently on building a new life and blocked out my family as much as I could. I found resources within me I hadn't known I had, and over time I developed a strong belief in my own talent. The more I put into my craft the better I felt about my work and myself. My self-esteem and my success grew hand in hand.

I made many new friends, most of them performers, and was always sharing my ideas with them about the many ways in which self-worth and success are intimately linked. Over time they started asking me to coach them for auditions, and soon my acting school at Carnegie Hall was born. I taught my own technique, along with how to market yourself in the industry. I began writing, directing, and producing plays as well, and my school blossomed into a vibrant artistic community.

As my life continued to evolve and flourish, in the back of my mind I was haunted by my sister's fate. She was still living with my mother and for the past twelve years had not left her spot on the couch except for one daily trip to the bathroom. My mother indulged her by serving her trays of junk food day and night. I couldn't imagine what would happen to her when my mother died. I secretly feared it.

When the day came that my mother fell ill and was taken to the hospital, Dolly bolted into the streets, alone in the world for the first time. I spoke with my mother in the hospital and tried to locate Dolly from New York, but to no avail. I had no clue where she might be or if she was okay.

Then one day, the phone rang and it was Dolly. She was reaching out to me for comfort—me, whom she had wanted to get rid of so long ago! She told me she was terrified of my mother dying, and she was now homeless. I ached for her vulnerability, and at the same time I feared being left with the responsibility of taking care of her for the rest of her life.

When Dolly called again a few days later with the news of my mother's death, I made a quick decision to go back to Los Angeles to bury my mother and help Dolly. I organized the funeral from New York and researched every possible avenue of housing for Dolly. Then, mustering up all my courage, I flew to Los Angeles.

Dolly wasn't strong enough to go to the funeral, so I didn't see her until afterwards. I was nervous as I drove to the temporary room she had found. When Dolly opened the door, I was shocked at the sight of her. All those years of eating junk food had taken their toll—she was obese and toothless. But I was touched by her brave dignity as she invited me in and offered me a chair. I tried to draw her out and comfort her, but she still wasn't comfortable talking. Soon I just turned to the task ahead.

I needed to get Dolly to go with me to see housing, but she was too frightened to leave her room. For the next five days I went without her and spent most of every day looking at every possible available apartment. But when I described them to her each night, for one reason or another, she rejected every one.

On my last day in Los Angeles I discovered a wonderful place and literally dragged Dolly to see it. It had its own entrance and was like a tiny, unique bungalow. It was not only clean, it was charming. I knew that Dolly could afford it with her disability check and my monthly help. She sat down on the bed and looked around, and I sensed that she liked it. Then the manager said, ". . . and your bathroom will be down the hall. You'll be sharing it with a very nice lady across the way."

Dolly shook her head and muttered, "No." She wouldn't share a bathroom. Period. I froze. She just kept shaking her head. Feeling helpless, I looked directly at her and said, "Dolly, I'm leaving for New York City tonight and then you're going to be on your own."

Suddenly, images of her living in a dangerous homeless shelter or wandering the streets flashed across my mind, and I started crying uncontrollably. "My worst fear has always been what would happen to you when Mother died!" I sobbed. "I just want you to be safe and okay." I slid to the floor beside her and cried and cried.

When I finally looked up, Dolly was staring at me in bewilderment. She said, "It's . . . hard . . . to absorb . . . that you care about me . . . that much." Then she very gently patted my arm. She took a deep breath, settled back onto the pillow on the bed, and I knew she'd stay.

We went to the Kmart a few miles away, and in a couple of hours I got her everything she would need. Back in her room, in a whirlwind of flying packages and swirling activity, I organized and decorated her new life. I made everything as beautiful as I could, finishing it off with one red rose and a picture of me by her bedside so she wouldn't feel alone.

She seemed dazed but slowly said, "I appreciate . . . your touch . . . on everything." I hugged her, and she hugged me back. And then I left her to begin again.

Now, over three years later, Dolly has her own life. She's still terrified, still suffering from anxiety attacks and phobias about everything, but less so. She might call me twenty-five times and hang up before I can pick up the phone. But when she's ready, our conversations are wonderful.

I wept twice at my sister's feet. The first time, it was for me, but the second time, it was for her. Something had grown inside me while I wasn't looking—love. And along with that has come a feeling of liberation I never imagined possible.

I got my revenge after all! I just never expected it to be so sweet.

Susan Brandis Slavin

Pause and Reflect

Name something that happened to you, or someone who wronged you or hurt you in your past (or present). Even if you are unable to make an amend directly, is it possible to forgive that person or situation within yourself?

LIFE LESSON #2:
PRACTICE ACCEPTANCE

God asks no man whether he will accept life.
That is not the choice.
You must take it. The only choice is how.

HENRY WARD BEECHER

Most of us have grown up in a world that teaches right from wrong. Parents, school teachers, and religious leaders are powerful influences that shape our opinions, our values, and our beliefs. Cultural traditions, regional customs, television, the Internet, friends, relatives, children, music—every day we are bombarded by thousands of pieces of input that contribute to our conditioning and the way we view life. Combine this conditioning with our genes, and you've got an answer for why you think, say, and do just about anything.

For example, I grew up in the black-and-white world of the South in the fifties and sixties. I was in the eleventh grade when my high school, Robert E. Lee High, was racially integrated. Police escorted the five history-making African-American students that first day of school in 1963. The majority of students kept their distance, but my conditioning was different from most. My mother had grown up in England in an environment of racial tolerance; my father had an innate sense of the equality of human beings and a marked lack of racial prejudice. The conditioning I received at home outweighed what I got at school—and I quickly found myself new friends.

But I was not completely free of prejudice. Years later, when I arrived in West Africa as a Peace Corps volunteer, I was strongly aware of being in the minority for the first time in my life. Then one day I noticed that the color of a person's skin no longer even registered in my brain. New conditioning had replaced old conditioning.

Conditioning can be hard to change, prejudices hard to drop. Differing values can strain families and friends—and tear a nation apart. We battle with our teens, who seem to view the world just a little differently from us. We find ourselves at odds with siblings with whom we have religious differences. And we have to avoid certain topics with friends for fear of stepping on toes and inviting confrontation.

But there's an extraordinary tool for remaining grounded and at peace in the face of differences: acceptance. Like forgiving, accepting someone does not mean that you agree with her. Nor does accepting a situation mean that you like it. Acceptance simply means recognizing that the person you're challenged by has different genes and conditioning from you. Or that the situation you're struggling with involves others' personal beliefs, which are as true for them as yours are for you.

Can you agree to disagree? Is it possible to let go of the belief that you're right and someone else is wrong? My peace and happiness have increased dramatically since I began practicing the words, "You could be right." Even when I'm *sure* I'm right, I practice saying these words, because it's true: they *could* be right.

The results of practicing acceptance have been profound for me. They include a distinct lack of tension in my body and mind, as well as an immediate opening for further dialogue when I admit that my way may not be The Way.

As for Catherine Rose, in the next story, her path to acceptance was long and difficult, but it was also profound. This story tackles a difficult but important theme for our times.

What Would Love Do?

One day, while I was working away at my desk deadlines and car pools and computers, a message flashed into my mind, clear, strong, and unmistakable: *You are going to have to disengage from all this, because soon you will need all your time and attention for something else.*

"All this" was quite a lot. I was mom to a lively nine-year-old boy, president of a publishing company, and editor and associate publisher of a regional magazine. I wrote a weekly newspaper column, was a Junior League volunteer, and Sunday school teacher. I taught meditation, traveled to courses and retreats, and sat on various community boards.

The message knocked me back into my chair. Then came the postscript, *If you don't spend more time with your son, you are going to miss his childhood.* For some reason, I believed it.

So I began to gradually dismantle and simplify my life, spending more time with my son. I realized how much I had been missing and was grateful for the message. I asked that God become my secretary and day-timer; it took about a year to get to a place where my day-timer was not already filled before the month began.

Toward the end of that year, my husband, Richard, and I were at the country home of friends. After dinner, Richard asked the hostess, "Would you mind if Catherine and I went out for a walk? We haven't had much of a chance to be together for a long time." Richard had an out-of-town office and was away a lot of the time.

After we had walked for a while in silence, Richard said, "I haven't been able to look you in the eyes for a long time, and after I tell you what I have to say, you may never want to speak to me again. You may want to get a lawyer first thing in the morning."

I froze inside. Richard stared at the ground for a few moments, then he said, "I've fallen in love with a man."

I went blank. I couldn't think. He said he had been spending a lot of time with gay friends in New Orleans and felt that he was bisexual. He went on for a long time, but I was oblivious of the time. My whole world was silently blasting apart.

In the following months, I was disoriented to a degree I had never known possible. But I was also surrounded by loving helpers, both seen and unseen, and felt the support of angelic presences literally holding me up. My son was my lifeline. I poured all the love from my broken heart into caring for him.

Richard was a rock, helping me through this trauma. For months I thought we could keep our family together and somehow make it work. We went to counselors, I read books, and asked a thousand questions about what being gay was all about.

Richard had known he was gay since he was five years old. He assumed he'd have to deny his natural feelings and find as much happiness as he could in a conventional life. When he fell in love and could no longer deny his feelings, he couldn't face either alternative: continuing to live a lie, or coming out with the truth.

Sometimes I felt compassion for his pain, and sometimes I

felt very betrayed. But I couldn't help seeing that Richard had always tried to be the best person he could be. I desperately didn't want to have to start my life over without him.

Four months after that walk, I hit my bottom point. I woke up in the middle of the night in deep despair, dark and painful beyond anything I'd ever experienced. After hours of agony, all I could think of was that death would be better than this torture, and many ways of killing myself flashed through my mind.

Just before dawn, in a pool of sweat, utterly exhausted, I called out seven times in a silent scream, *Help me, help me, oh God, help me.* Then I finally fell into a numb sleep.

At eight o'clock that morning, the phone began to ring. A parade of my dearest friends and family members called to say, "Are you okay?" and "I was just thinking about you and wondering how you are doing." Several of them were people I rarely spoke to because they lived far away. There were seven calls—one for each of my cries for help. Clearly, I had never been alone and without help, even in that dark pit of torment.

From that day, though still quite tender and wounded, I began to feel more and more centered. Slowly I began to pull myself together and move forward. As I grew stronger, I began to seriously doubt that my idea to stay together was workable.

One evening, standing in my kitchen pantry, I heard

another message. This one was decidedly more light-hearted. *Catherine, you can stay married, but it will be much more difficult than is necessary.* And then almost chuckling, it said, *Honey, you're gonna have your cake and eat it too.* At that point I knew that I could keep all the love we had—and still move on.

In time Richard moved to an apartment nearby. Stephen, our son, could ride over on his bicycle, and we all stayed very close. Soon after our divorce, I moved away to go back to school, and Richard moved to the Northwest. Stephen went to live with him when he was fourteen.

I thought at the time that my "piece of cake" perfect new man might be just around the corner. For over fifteen years I looked, and watched, and waited, trying to make something happen. Finally, I let go of that desire and felt the most glorious freedom. Soon after, a beautiful, loving relationship opened up to me.

Looking back, I can see the perfection. Those fifteen years let me heal from the trauma and begin my life anew based on honesty as well as love. I outgrew the last stabs of resentment. I saw the deeper wisdom that provided Richard, Stephen, my new husband, and me with just the right opportunities at just the right moments. We all grew, and our love grew too.

We still get together for holidays, birthdays, and family trips. Our loving family has expanded to include a man who shares Richard's life. I call him my husband-in-law! And this Christmas, sixteen years since it all began, my new life partner will join our family gathering. Love was there in the beginning, the middle, and the end of this great shift in my life. I'm just glad I had the heads-up warning, and had already turned my day-timer over to God. He made all the appointments for me. I just had to show up.

Catherine Rose

Pause and Reflect

1. Think of someone you know whose religious or political viewpoint is dramatically opposed to yours. Can you accept that person's right to his/her beliefs, even though they don't mesh with yours? Can you agree to disagree?
2. Practice saying these words: "You could be right."

LIFE LESSON #3:
HIP-HOP PAST YOUR JUDGMENTS

The difference between a weed
and a flower is a judgment.

ANONYMOUS

There's a big difference between a preference and a judgment.

A preference is a natural liking or disliking of someone or something. Judging is the act of labeling something we don't like as "bad" or "wrong." What differentiates judgments from preferences is emotion. You may prefer chocolate over vanilla, but choosing your flavor doesn't require a huge emotional decision. On the other hand, judgments are often accompanied by strong feelings like anger, blame, superiority, or resentment.

The minute you take a position *against* something, you can feel the "emotional charge" in your body. It can show up as a need to quickly, urgently lash out at someone who's said something threatening. It can result in an e-mail you later wish you hadn't sent. It can arise as anger, worry, guilt, or sadness.

But here's the thing: emotions are natural; holding on to them is not. It's normal to feel hurt if your best friend says something mean about you. It's natural to feel angry if someone else gets the promotion you thought you deserved. But you will be able to move mountains if you do this simple thing: wait until the emotional charge has dissipated before you act or say anything.

Is it a sign of fear or weakness not to speak up for yourself right away? It could be. But sometimes it takes time to really get in touch with our feelings and what's behind them. More often than not, speaking up for yourself is far more powerful when you've stayed with your feelings until they're resolved within yourself, or at least until you've regained objectivity or equilibrium. Then you have the choice to speak—or not speak.

This happened to me after a contributor to a book I was working on had just signed off on minor edits I had made to her story. The next day, the piece *I had asked her to write* appeared in her weekly on-line newsletter! I felt angry for a little while, and I kept thinking about how I could politely tell her that it would have been *really* nice if she had waited until after my book came out before publishing it elsewhere! I even started an e-mail.

But recognizing that seeing "my" story had "activated" me, I resolved to do nothing until my emotions had subsided. I realized I was really mad at myself for not having thought to ask her to wait. By the time the "charge" disappeared, I no longer felt the need to say anything to her. I still might, but if I do, it will be to communicate genuinely, without trying to make her wrong.

In the next story, Yaniyah Pearson was able to "hip-hop past her judgments" to discover, as we've seen in previous Life Lessons, that beneath the surface, we're all more alike than different, and that spirit unites.

 ## The Beat

It was going to be a long drive. With four young adults packed into my car, I was headed to Washington, D.C. to join 125 young people at the YouthBuild and AmeriCorp National Young Leaders Conference.

After five years of directing the YouthBuild program in Brooklyn, New York, I was thrilled to be making this trip. YouthBuild is a national program that provides high school dropouts with on-the-job and leadership training in home construction and renovation for their communities.

But my enthusiasm was tempered by some anxiety. What would we talk about? What kind of music would we listen to? I knew they would prefer rap and hip-hop, which I found to be materialistic, crude, and downright offensive. Although I enjoy drumming circles, moved by the beat of powerful drums, I couldn't relate to the hip-hop/rap beat. In the minority, however, I surrendered to their choices.

Half an hour into the trip, I felt isolated and trapped,

battered by the music's sounds and rhymes, the "N word," derogatory names for women, glorification of violence, and greed. With no way to escape, I took a deep breath and thought about the gap between us.

Until now, I hadn't truly felt the weight of the cultural differences between the YouthBuild teens and myself. Although we were all African-Americans, I had been blessed with the opportunities that come from growing up in a safe neighborhood and getting a college education.

My YouthBuild teens had none of these advantages. They were high school dropouts, struggling with poverty, gangs, and substance abuse. I was dedicated to their success in life, but I was under no illusions about the gulf between our realities and worldviews. Sometimes it limited my ability to more deeply connect.

I realized I didn't usually try to bridge this gap with my students. I took the authority role: they had to learn to do things my way if they wanted a better future. They had to reach out to me, change their language patterns, and endure criticisms of their value system. My "policy" weighed heavily on me. So did my distress from the incessant beat, by now becoming intolerable.

Then one of the boys loaded a new cassette and some of my favorite soul music filled the car. I relaxed. From that moment we bonded, singing, joking, and sharing our strategies for the conference.

When the meeting began, my role was to support the young leaders in charge. As the day went on, I realized that I was on pure "love" duty. All I needed to do was listen and show compassion to the tense staff and the young leaders who were carrying everything on their shoulders.

As the conference progressed, the bonding I had experienced with my students during our trip expanded. I felt more deeply connected with others than ever before. During conflicts between staff and youth leaders, I stayed focused and nonreactionary. I was sought out both by young people to work through occasional discontent and disillusionment and by staff leaders looking to relax.

It dawned on me that I was responding to life in a profoundly different way. The love generated by this incredible gathering sprinkled me with tenderness and joy. I was in love with everyone.

As my heart grew fuller, I thought I would explode with emotion. I needed a release. Music! I needed music! All we had done for two days was talk.

On the last night my wish came true. We were invited to an Up with People! concert sponsored by another group at our hotel. Young international performers fused national/traditional songs and modern American music. The influence of African-American hip-hop culture—music despised and condemned by much of America—was indisputable. The jubilation of those young people listening to the street music performed by people from all over the world brought tears to my eyes.

Afterward, filled with the experience, I went for a short walk. An ethnically diverse group of ten young men from the conference were huddled in a circle, free-styling. This improvisational rhyming contest is a central component of hip-hop/rap musical culture. Suddenly I wanted to experience their world as one of them.

Slowly, I inched my way into the circle. I found myself swaying in unison to the "beats," the percussive, rhythmic, guttural sounds of two young men. Whenever one of the rappers was inspired to rhyme, he would step into the center of the circle. When he was done, another immediately jumped in and took his place.

The vibration of the circle pulsated throughout my body. The beats took me into a trance-like state, completely connected, safe, secure. Negative lyrics didn't feel any different from positive ones—all exuded love.

Swaying and lost in the rhythm, I was reminded of my drumming circles. For the first time, I could relate the spirituality of my music and theirs. Both had the power in the beat. But this young group also had the power of language and the harmony it created.

As curfew approached, the circle finally broke up with smiles, back slaps, and high fives. I felt both embraced and invisible, which seemed appropriate. I had done nothing to earn entrance into their circle except surrender myself to the same currents that moved their spirits.

That night, I couldn't sleep. I wanted to write. Although I hadn't had the nerve to rhyme in the circle, a kaleidoscope of words was circling in my mind. Lyrics came as one more gift. I sat up and composed.

The next morning when asked to share reflections, I rushed to the front of the room and recited my verses in dedication to the free-styling brothers. As I spoke, they began to accompany me with the beats, the truest sign of recognition they could have given me.

Looking back on that night, I am grateful I could cross cultural barriers, removing the illusion of separation. The very music I had hated on the drive became a vehicle to connect in love and unite in spirit. As I wrote:

Truth is—that we share rhythms, vibrations,
connections to a beat. A universal beat that ain't even old,
because it has always been here.
There has always been a beat here, in my heart,
in the heart of the ancestors,
in the heart of the Mother, our Mother Earth,
and even before Her birth, there was the beat—
like the breath of God—permeating all the universes.

Yaniyah Pearson

Pause and Reflect

1. Has anybody pushed your buttons lately? Can you let go of your position for a moment and see the situation from their point of view?
2. Reflect for a moment on Victor Frankl's words. Here was a man who survived a concentration camp by finding the good in everyone, including his captors. He said, "Everything can be taken from a man but one thing, the last of the human freedoms: to choose one's attitude in any given set of circumstances, to choose one's own way." Is there any aspect of your life that might be served by a change in your attitude?

Life Lesson #4:
Be the Change

> *If you are distressed by anything external, the pain is not due to the thing itself but to your own estimate of it, and this you have the power to revoke at any moment.*
>
> Marcus Aurelius

Almost everyone has ideas about how to change the world. We all want it to be a better place, even if we differ about how to bring about change. Sometimes we rail against the government or against large corporations, seeing only greed and corruption in high places. We might get extremely angry about all the injustice in the world, and think, *If I were in charge, things would be very different.* But would they? No doubt righteous anger has its place in life, but perhaps we might also remember that real change has to start within each of us. If we want to change the world, we must first change ourselves.

In Hawaii there is a technique known as *ho'oponopono.* One doctor who practiced *ho'oponopono* succeeded in curing a hospital ward of criminally insane patients without ever meeting them in person. Instead, he reviewed each person's file and then turned inward, into his own heart. He kept saying, over and over again, "I'm sorry," and "I love you."

We might think, well that sounds nice, but how could it possibly have any effect? The curious thing is that it did. After a few months, some patients who had been shackled were allowed to walk unrestricted. Others improved so much they were taken off their medications. Some who had been considered "lifers" were freed.

The doctor explained that in *ho'oponopono,* he recognized that the people around him were reflections of something that needed to be healed in himself. Situations and events involving others may appear as something outside ourselves, but the truth according to *ho'oponopono* is that the world is as we are, and that if we want to heal it we must take complete responsibility for ourselves and our connection to the world around us.[1]

The story is told about a famous rabbi who lived in Europe several hundred years ago. One day he encountered a man breaking the Jewish law by working on the Sabbath. But instead of remonstrating with the man, the rabbi decided that he would examine himself. *What is it about me,* he asked himself, *that causes me to encounter someone who is working on the Sabbath?*

Most of us are not used to thinking like this. We are accustomed to seeing ourselves as separate from the world around us, in which case it is easy to assign blame to others for any problem at all, from noisy neighbors to a war halfway across the globe. Perhaps we might consider the possibility that everything that comes into our lives, both good and bad, is a reflection, a mirror in which to see ourselves. If we accept such a radical premise, we might find new meaning in the words of the song that is heard in so many churches today: "Let there be peace on earth, and let it begin with me."

There is no other place to start.

☕ Moment of Truth

It was one of the largest student rallies in the history of the antiwar movement in Boston. Thousands of students flowed down Commonwealth Avenue, more swelling the ranks every moment. Large placards swayed above the moving tide of humanity: The Resistance, SDS, End the War, Get Out of Vietnam, Make Love Not War, and so on.

It was 1969, and I was a graduate student at Boston University School of Theology, Martin Luther King Jr.'s alma mater. As the civil rights and antiwar movements merged, it became increasingly difficult to be an academic when a revolution was taking place on the streets of the nation.

My opposition to the conflict in Southeast Asia had deep roots. As a child in England, I had listened to the stories of my aunts, uncles, and grandparents, who were still recovering from the trauma of the First World War. I learned of the trenches, the mud, the gas, and the death of husbands, brothers, sons, and my grandfather, even as we huddled in bomb shelters with another world war raging around us.

Such events have a profound effect on young minds. I had a deep abhorrence for war; to me, it was an act of utter futility. As a pacifist, I did not believe in violence to resolve the difficulties and disagreements that beset human beings. So when the Vietnam conflict came along, I took a stand. In Boston, with one of the largest student populations of any city in the world, opposition to the war was fierce.

It was a warm, sunny day as we marched to the Boston Common. Despite the serious purpose, it was a festive occasion. Side streets served as tributaries to the large noisy river of humanity as it flowed toward the heart of Boston. Reaching the intersection where the road from Harvard and MIT crossed the river, we saw students as far as the eye could see. We believed the "warmongers" in Washington would have to listen to us. Our numbers were simply too large to ignore.

As I approached the Commons I immediately felt concerned. I noticed police on horseback, on motorcycles, on foot, and with leashed German shepherds. The presence of military vehicles was an added worry. Troop carriers and

Jeeps were parked on side streets; the National Guard had been called out.

The Common was full. A bright ocean of humanity covered every blade of grass and overflowed; even the trees were filled with students. The numbers far exceeded the expectations of those of us who'd spent weeks organizing demonstrations all across the country. Was it fifty thousand, a hundred thousand? We couldn't tell. For hours we sat listening as speakers addressed the crowd—student leaders, political leaders, and faculty members from many universities—all advocating peace, not war. The last speaker, aware of the danger around us, urged that we return to our respective universities in a peaceful manner. To resort to violence, he argued, would discredit what we were about.

The crowd began to move, trying to disperse, only to find they couldn't. Police and National Guard now surrounded us. Some students tried to break through their ranks only to find themselves under attack. The smell of tear gas permeated the air.

Trying to escape the violence, we crossed the Common as quickly as we could. I noticed ahead of me a young longhaired student in his early twenties. From the corner of my eye I also noticed a policeman approaching from behind and to my right. He was twirling a long wooden nightstick, and his eyes seemed riveted on the longhaired student.

Catching up to him he grabbed his club in both hands and drove it into the young man's back. I heard the breaking of bones as the student dropped like a sack of potatoes.

Something deep within me snapped, and I moved toward the policeman, fully intent on killing him. I experienced a sense of great lucidity, aware of both my thoughts and actions as if I were observing someone else.

A momentary hesitation dominated the deadly rage I felt as I approached him from behind. In the same instant that I moved toward him I knew I wouldn't get away with the killing. There were people everywhere. I would spend a good portion of my life in jail, might even be executed for what I was about to do.

Then, suddenly, something opened up and I saw myself as never before. I, a pacifist, someone unalterably opposed to violence, was fully capable of killing another human being. For years I'd taken pride in being better than others. How often had I pointed fingers at those who justified violence and war?

One moment more and I'd have stepped into a yawning chasm from which there would be no turning back. I was stunned. I was capable of killing; I was no better than those I protested against. Not knowing myself had almost cost the life of another human being and caused untold suffering for his family and mine.

In that lucid state I knew I needed to understand myself.

In so doing I would understand human nature, for as I had seen, I was no different from anyone else. In those few seconds on Boston Common I'd found the roots of war. Now it was time to discover the origin of peace.

Colin D. Mallard

Pause and Reflect

1. Do you ever find yourself reacting strongly to what someone says or does? Reflect for a moment on whether that person's behavior is something you, too, might be capable of.

2. If someone is expressing anger toward you, ask yourself what is being reflected for you. If someone is expressing generosity, what does that say about you? Do the same exercise with three types of behavior you notice being mirrored back to you from people in your environment.

3. Are you in any relationship right now that's uncomfortable? What is being mirrored to you?

FAITH, GRACE, AND MIRACLES

There is a crack in everything
That's how the light gets in.

Leonard Cohen

LIFE LESSON #1:
KEEP THE FAITH

Faith is the bird that knows dawn,
and sings while it is still dark.

TAGORE

If you're old enough to have watched *The Ozzie and Harriet Show,* the popular television program of the late fifties, you probably saw actresses Sara Buckner (now O'Meara) and Yvonne Lime (now Fedderson). They had feature roles on the show as Ricky and David Nelson's girlfriends. Real-life best friends and roommates, Sara and Yvonne had plans for big careers in Hollywood.

When they auditioned for an entertainment tour of Korea and Japan, they were selected out of 500 girls because they looked like "the girls next door." The story you are about to read tells of an experience they had in Japan that changed their lives—and, ultimately, the lives of thousands of children.

Sara and Yvonne say they owe their success to faith. In their case, faith is connected to their understanding that they are never in charge of what they are doing—"God is."

But faith is not necessarily religious, nor does it necessarily have to do with belief. Dr. James W. Fowler III, a Harvard-trained expert in the psychology of religion and the author of *Stages of Faith*, says that faith is a person's way of making sense of life. He says that everyone operates by some basic faith, whether it is associated with religion or not.

For example, I experience faith as a feeling of being at home in the universe, an undeniable knowing that all is well and that all will be taken care of. For me, faith means living in a reality that sees everything that happens as having a purpose, and everything that happens to me personally, good or bad, as contributing to my understanding about life. As my friend Father Tom Miller puts it, "Darkness is my candle."

For my sister, faith is not merely having hope—it is absolute belief. She describes her faith in God as something that can release burdens and worries, and that has helped her keep her sanity time and time again. She says that faith is "a condition of the heart in which you have no doubts, but rather certainty and trust. Faith erases anxiety and doubt, and creates or builds inner peace and happiness."

In the case of Sara and Yvonne, they say faith allows them to put one foot in front of the other toward every next goal, always knowing that, on the other side of obstacles, there are miracles.

☕ Silence Broken

Yvonne and I were safe in our hotel room in Tokyo, Japan, after four days of the worst typhoon the city had ever seen. For a couple of nights, we had sat in darkness without power as the winds pounded at our windows. We had been under strict orders not to leave the hotel, but at the first sign of clearing we decided to venture out. Our youthful curiosity fueled our sense of adventure.

We were amazed at the devastation. Trash and debris were scattered everywhere; mud oozed up over our shoes. The stench almost took our breath away.

We walked for about a mile, and had just decided to turn back, when we suddenly came upon some small children huddled together, trying to fend off the freezing winds. They were shivering and crying; their knuckles were bleeding from the cold; their light clothing was torn and soaked. We counted eleven of them, ranging from about two to twelve years old.

Horrified, we unbuttoned our coats and beckoned them to come and get warm. Our coats ballooned as they squeezed under them. We knew what we had to do and began shuffling back toward our hotel, sure we could find out where these children belonged.

With a couple of children in our arms and others clinging

to our coats, we boldly walked the children through the hotel lobby, hoping no one would stop us. The maids looked at us curiously. Safely in our room, we closed the door, looked at each other and said, "Now what?" We had no plan, so we just did the next thing that seemed natural.

We bathed the children and wrapped them in makeshift clothing. Then we called room service and were surprised when the order came with plates, glasses, and utensils for thirteen people! The whole hotel was abuzz about the two women and eleven children.

We approached the colonel appointed to oversee our tour about what to do. Surely, we thought, the parents of these children must be looking for them. The colonel hit the roof, but we refused to abandon the children. Finally, he relented and told us to find an orphanage to take them to. He ushered us to a taxi with an English-speaking driver.

For two days we went from orphanage to orphanage, but were told there was no room. It was early afternoon of the second day when we approached the last orphanage on our list. When we ushered the children out of the taxi, we were surprised when they started pulling back and crying in unison.

We were greeted by a gentle-looking man who looked surprised when he saw the children. He spoke to our driver-translator, who informed us that the children had been living in this very orphanage before they were sent into the streets.

"How could this be?" we asked.

Our driver explained that the children were half-American and half-Japanese. Because of the typhoon, so many Japanese had been left homeless that the government could not subsidize any mixed-blood children.

We were stunned—and then enraged. These children had become "throwaways." They had no value, not even to their parents.

We returned to the hotel, where next we were directed to a Japanese woman known as "Mama Kin," already known for having taken mixed-blood children into her home. We loaded the children into the van and struck out to find her.

Mama Kin's one-room hut had no front door in the doorway. The windows had no windowpanes. She wanted to help but pointed to the ten orphans for whom she was caring already. She explained that she had no money to take care of them, much less to take in more.

We learned that Mama Kin's children had been turned away by their families, and she had turned this dirt-floor shack into a refuge. We could see she was filled with love and told her if she would help us, we would help the other children. Finally, she agreed to keep our children, and we promised to return the next day.

Yvonne and I decided we would ask for help from the

servicemen attending our show that evening. We weren't sure what might happen when we spoke about these half-American children, but we had to take that chance.

That night, we could hardly concentrate on our performance. When it was over, our hearts pounded as we explained the situation.

"Some of these might be your children," we said. "Please, won't you help these innocent little Amerasian orphans?"

We pleaded with them to meet us at our hotel the next morning.

The response was fantastic. More than a dozen soldiers arrived in an army truck filled with blankets, C-rations, and lumber. We spent the entire day at Mama Kin's. Some of the servicemen put in a front door and windowpanes, while others accompanied us to a market to buy bedding, tatami mats, warm clothes, and food. These kind men cared. For the rest of our tour, we continued to help the homeless Amerasian children and the kind-faced woman who had dedicated her life to housing them.

As word got out, more Amerasian children were left on the doorstep of Mama Kin's hut with notes that read, "For the Orphanage of Mixed Blood." Mama Kin's home became our first orphanage, housing more than 100 children after the renovations, which we were able to pull out of thin air—with God's help. That began our journey of building and maintaining three more orphanages in Tokyo. At this point in time, we officially established ourselves as International Orphans, Inc., and although we faced many obstacles along the way, we knew we were not alone because we had dedicated this mission to God.

By 1964 virtually all Amerasian orphans in Japan had found homes, and we thought our work was done. But then Congress asked if we could help the orphaned children in Vietnam in establishing orphanages. Through International Orphans, Inc., we raised funds to build five orphanages, schools, and a children's hospital there. When U.S. troops pulled out of Vietnam, we helped organize Operation Babylift to rescue the Amerasian orphans who would likely be killed if left behind.

Then Nancy Reagan asked if we would turn our attention to the plight of child abuse in America. We didn't want to believe it existed, but through our organization Childhelp, we answered the call and continue to work on behalf of children today.

We know that in all our projects, we have God by our side, along with some special "earthly angels." We keep putting one foot in front of the other toward our next goal, with faith, prayer, and trust. We have gone from obstacle to miracle, knowing that somehow, the miracle will show up on the other side of the obstacle. We have remembered that we are not in charge, God is.

We know this is what God wants us to do. Someone has to give these children a voice. And it's our privilege to continue to do so.

Sara O'Meara and Yvonne Fedderson

Pause and Reflect

1. What does faith mean to you?
2. Does faith play a role in the way you live.

LIFE LESSON #2:
BE AWAKE TO GRACE

Everything has its wonders, even darkness and
silence, and I learn, whatever state
I may be in, therein to be content.

HELEN KELLER

Grace is a mysterious and unexpected experience of understanding, acceptance, surrender, recognition, or resolution. It is a gift of exceeding worth.

When I traveled around the world for a year after leaving West Africa, I had hundreds of memorable encounters with people, places, and animals. But two stand out as moments of the purest grace imaginable. Both had to do with the natural world.

I was in Nepal, in a beautiful valley called Pokhara. The first clear day, I rented a small rowboat and paddled out to the middle of Lake Pokhara, where I lay on my back taking in the magnificent Annapurna Mountains, the front range of the Himalayas. I stayed there all day, watching the light change on the face of the mountains as the sun moved across the sky.

On the return trip to Katmandu, as I sat squashed in the center of the back seat of a taxi between two Nepalese, the hairs on the back of my neck suddenly rose, and my spine started tingling. Something made me turn around—and I found myself looking directly at Mount Everest for the first time. My mind stopped for a moment, and then I cried. The beauty and the majesty of the world's highest peak transmitted to me an experience of the divine, touching a place within me that I had not known before.

The second experience happened soon after that. I left Katmandu on a bus headed for Varanasi, the holiest city of India. I wanted to see the famous Ganges River for the first time.

Our bus traveled all day and night, arriving in Varanasi well before dawn. In the darkness, I made my way toward the river, asking directions of people already awake in the streets. I found a *ghat,* a series of steps leading down to the river. Sensing I was close, I set my bags on one of the steps and sat down, settling in to wait for the sun to rise.

I could hear the sounds of the river lapping at the steps. As dawn approached, I could hear other sounds of water being poured; eventually I could see the faint outline of a man standing in the water in his *dhoti,* performing morning prayers and ablutions. Around 5:00 AM, the first rays of the morning unveiled the River Ganges. As I watched the light on the rippling gold and black water before me, my mind and body settled into a state of perfect stillness. I felt the greatest peace I had ever known. It was another moment of grace, in which the experience of what is holy is revealed.

Even the everyday sense of the word implies an element of the divine: a graceful dancer, a powerful athlete, a great piece of art, or the music of Beethoven. Surely divine inspiration has touched them all.

But grace takes many forms. The ability to make sense out of tragedy is a certain kind of grace. To love and be loved is grace, as is anything that brings a measure of peace. We cannot claim it or demand it. And we must be awake to notice it when it happens.

The next story, by Nancy Bellmer, is an example not only of noticing grace, but also of how to receive it and use it fully in the way we live our lives.

Bathed in Light

We almost lost him before he was born.

In 1982, seven months into my pregnancy with my son Braden, I was taken to the hospital in Reno, Nevada. My husband, Rick, and I learned that I had an amniotic leak and a baby who weighed only three pounds.

The doctors told us that I needed to carry Braden as long as I could, so I began taking even greater care of myself, focusing on keeping my baby inside me. After thirty-seven weeks, he was born. He weighed only four pounds, eight ounces, but he was vibrant and healthy. To us, he was perfect.

As Braden grew, our friends described him as blissful, saying he looked as if he "walked on air." When he was one-and-a-half years old, we moved to a small community in the Midwest, where his constant joy and delight affected everyone he met.

In June 1984, when Braden was just over two years old, a friend from Tahoe came to visit. She brought her son, who was a year older than Braden, and the boys loved playing together.

One night during our friend's visit, Braden began crying from a bad dream. I went into his room to comfort him. "Owie, owie, hurt head," he cried repeatedly.

The next morning Rick remarked about a dream he'd had. He was driving a white Mercedes and hit and killed a teenaged boy. He saw the boy's twin on the side of the road, which he interpreted as the boy's soul. Rick wondered why he would have dreamed such a thing.

Then we both got ready for work. Rick sat in the driveway in the seat of his delivery-sized work van, going over some paperwork. I was in the kitchen, while my friend stood in the doorway talking to me and keeping an eye on the boys, who were playing outside on their tricycles. When Rick was ready to leave, he noticed the boys were eating watermelon on the porch. He put his paperwork away, looked in both rearview mirrors, and backed out.

But every parent knows how quickly children can move. In one of those irretrievable flashes of time, Braden had gotten back on his tricycle, pedaled alongside the truck and was behind it when Rick backed out.

I heard Braden's cry and ran to him. His soul waited just long enough for me to reach him and take his hand in mine before he slipped away.

At that instant, I experienced a deep stillness. I was filled with an enormous light that enveloped me, inside and out, and I knew that my longstanding desire for a direct experience of God had been fulfilled. The light was so overpowering that it dwarfed the feeling of shock and loss. I felt supported and protected. The pain was there, but it was only a small part of my experience. The light also gave me the experience of complete acceptance and surrender—and compassion for Rick, who was in unspeakable agony as we both held our little boy. All through the next hour, in the midst of the physical and emotional shock and the arrival of emergency vehicles, I remained completely enveloped by the light.

After Braden's body was taken away, Rick and I went into Braden's room to meditate. We both had the experience of Braden's spirit in the form of a pinkish light, and heard these words: "I'm fine; I'm free." We also remembered the two dreams, which gave us a strong sense of prophecy, the feeling that what had happened was beyond our control and our limited understanding.

That evening, when our kind neighbors brought over dinner, I had my first experience of the huge contrast between what was happening inside me and the mundane details of "getting on" with life. I remember thinking, *If I eat this, this is what I will be filling my emptiness and loss with.* At the same time, I felt buoyant, blissful, light-filled.

In the following weeks, even in my deep sadness, I felt filled with love. When friends came to visit, I found myself comforting them. Although they had been unsure of what to say in the face of such a loss, something of my expanded internal state seemed to touch them and they left feeling transformed.

I definitely had questions, especially, *Why?* At times I felt confused and sad. But I never felt angry, either with Rick or God.

Over the next six weeks, Rick and I both had powerful experiences of Braden. One image was of an angelic child. Another was of him as a princely young adult. The last experience was of Braden as an old soul, with flowing beard and robes, floating in the air, leading a group of heavenly beings. This was the last "visit" we would have, and through it all, the message was clear: our lives and our souls were not separate; Braden was—and would always be—with us.

Yet when the visits ceased, we found that we deeply wanted to have another child, not to replace Braden but to give us the opportunity to parent again. As we looked toward the birth of a new child, our previous loss became easier to accept.

My pregnancy with our second child, Shane, was smooth, as was his delivery; he arrived within two hours. And our third child, Saralyn, rushed out in forty-five minutes!

When I reflect on what happened in June 1984, I feel that the grace I experienced as Braden died was a gift often given, but not always perceived. On the surface, there was the tragedy of our child's death, but there was also the presence of the light, the grace of God. It made me aware that there is always more than what appears on the surface. I now believe that grace is always available to us, if we can just be open to its presence.

This year, Rick and I will celebrate our twenty-fifth wedding anniversary, nineteen years after Braden's passing. A couple of years ago I attended the graduation of the class that would have been Braden's. It was sweet—I felt as if I were their mother, too. I wept, not from sadness at Braden's absence, but with the tears that come from such poignant moments and the knowledge that Braden had already shared his own special graduation with us so many years ago.

There are two sides to our experience: human and

divine. When we are truly awake to the divine, grace dissolves every challenge we face. This wisdom about life is a part of that enormous light that has remained with me. I consider it Braden's greatest gift.

Nancy Bellmer

Pause and Reflect

Have you ever experienced something that felt like divine intervention? Do you feel your life is touched by grace in a general way? Do you believe that grace is something that just happens, or that we can draw it to us though a certain way of living and being?

LIFE LESSON #3:
FIND YOUR INNER REFUGE

True self is the part of us that does not change when circumstances do.

MASON COOLEY

When I was in the Peace Corps in West Africa, the English language books in the Peace Corps' library in Cotonou were highly prized by us volunteers. One day on a trip to my country's capital, I pulled a copy of Hermann Hesse's *Siddhartha* off the shelves and took it home to devour.

I was deeply struck by Siddhartha's words: ". . . inside of you, there is a peace and refuge, to which you can go at every hour of the day and be at home . . ." This book awakened in me a great longing for such peace, and so, instead of reenlisting for a third year in Africa, I decided to travel to India, the site of Siddartha, in search of someone who might help me find it.

My journey continues to this day, and it has been glorious! Sometimes I feel I have found everything I ever wanted, and sometimes I still long for more. Have I found inner peace? I'm not sure I could say that I was at peace recently when I spent eight hours in an emergency room in Toronto waiting to see if my eye symptoms indicated a detached retina!

(They didn't, thank God.) Or when my husband and I decided to live halfway across the country from each other to pursue our creative dreams. (We're now divorced.)

But underlying the ups and downs of life, behind the swings between joy and despair, I recognize that within myself is a place of refuge, a part of me that does not change, the eternal aspect of life that is within me, and that I am within. Whatever part of the cycle of life I find myself in, up or down, I know that "this too shall pass"—because that is the nature of life. And the more I accept *everything* that happens in my life as simply part of the experience of being human, the freer I become.

This is exactly what happened to Lindy Jones. I ran into Lindy one morning at yoga. It was the first time we had seen each other since her partner, Matthew, had passed away from cancer in the Philippines four months earlier. We held each other for a long time. I learned she was planning a road trip south to visit her family. Her first stop would be New Orleans, to carry cameras around the annual Jazz Festival for her father, a documentary photographer. I told her it was hard to believe I had grown up in Louisiana and never been to Jazz Fest. She unhesitatingly replied, "Come on down! You can stay with me."

Lindy is an extraordinary woman and a great singer/songwriter. I was excited about spending some time with her and meeting her family. But as we enjoyed Jazz Fest together, sharing mango ices and big bowls of shrimp étouffée, I gradually realized she was just going through the motions. On the surface she seemed happy, loving, and interested in the people and events going on around her. But inside, the grief she was experiencing at the loss of her partner was overwhelming, and she had lost the desire to live. By the end of our time together, I knew she was in a place of deep despair.

A couple of months later, when I invited Lindy to stay at my house in the Midwest, I found a different person from the woman I had spent time with in New Orleans. She was happy, vibrant, and alive. Life seemed to flow through her in a way that felt magical to me. We came and went comfortably around each other, and at moments the day would throw us together unexpectedly. One night we found ourselves at midnight lying on a blanket on the golf course down the street from my house, looking at stars and fireflies. And we finally had time for the story of Matthew.

I think it confirms that there is a place of refuge within us—that it is possible to know peace regardless of how great the pain or intense the pleasure in our lives.

A Star-Filled Night

I had been with Matthew for a year and a half when he was diagnosed with gastric cancer and told he had one to two months to live. Having been advised that any Western medical approach would likely be futile at this point, we flew to the Philippines to see the renowned psychic surgeons there. A friend of ours had been cured of cancer by these surgeons five years before. Since then, he had advised ten friends to go there, seven of whom are now in remission.

Matthew was one of the three who didn't make it. When he died, I was left facing not only the grief of losing my beloved, but also the challenge of dealing with his death in a foreign country. I argued with officials to let me stay with his body when it was taken to the morgue. I traveled in the tropical heat with his body two hours to the nearest crematorium. I sat next to the furnace for the six hours it took for his remains to be cremated. I found myself asking the question, *What's real?*

After the cremation, I went back to our apartment in Baguio City and threw myself into preparing a sacred space for Matthew's ashes. I took everything out of the room, turned the beds on end, washed the floors and the bathroom. Then I poured lavender oil over the parquet floor and rubbed it in on my hands and knees. I put the beds back down and put fresh linens on them, lit candles and incense, and sprinkled rose petals over the beds and floor. It felt like a purifying ritual for both of us. Friends called, but I cherished the time I spent alone in ceremony of Matthew's passing.

I found a beautiful ebony urn for the ashes and hired a local craftsman to carve the words "Into Love and Light" on the inside of the lid, along with the dates of Matthew's birth and death. The Filipinos touched me deeply with their quiet, heartfelt sincerity and sympathy.

Finally, it was time to return to the States, and I needed official documents to take the ashes home. I contacted the American embassy in Manila and was told to be there at 7:00 AM the day of my flight to California. It was a grueling trip to Manila, managing six pieces of luggage—mine and Matthew's—plus a wheelchair.

I arrived at the embassy as instructed, only to find it closed for Martin Luther King Jr. Day. A guard told me no one was there who could help me. Fighting hysteria, I begged him to call the official who had told me to be there on that day and time. With a flood of relief, I saw compassion in the guard's eyes and realized he was going to help me. Ultimately, the woman I had spoken with and her supervisor came in on their day off and began the paperwork.

For five hours I sat in the courtyard, holding the urn with Matthew's ashes in my lap. I was surprised to find that I didn't feel restless. I asked myself if there was anything I'd rather be doing. Watching a movie? Sitting in a café? I realized that I wouldn't want to be anywhere else at that moment, which was perfect as it was. Even though from one perspective everything was terribly wrong, I felt the deeper truth that everything was exactly as it should be.

That evening I flew to California, Matthew's home for most of his life. I felt numb and depressed, but I had promised Matthew to take care of his affairs and spread his ashes on Mount Tamalpais. I stayed with a friend and did my best to function normally, but my life felt empty and pointless.

A few weeks later, I climbed a steep path with a group of Matthew's family and friends to a place near the summit of Mount Tam. The light on the Pacific Ocean was shimmering and radiant, and we talked about how Matthew had changed our lives. As we shared our stories, the day went through many changes—misty, clear, darkening, sunny. It was the most beautiful spot I had ever seen, and we all felt Matthew's presence.

A month later I walked through the door of Matthew's house in Iowa. I looked around the room. There were the chairs we had sat in at the kitchen table; there were the beans he had used to make coffee. I sat down and pain washed through me. I would have to live without Matthew, and the thought was unbearable. At forty, I had finally found a relationship that worked. I couldn't accept that he was gone.

The days went by but I didn't care about them. I wanted to die. One morning I was curled up on the living room floor, aching with sadness. Suddenly, I dropped into what seemed to be a well of grief. I began to feel deeply into it and discovered that it wasn't what I had thought. I had a visceral experience of the poignancy and mystery of life, the depth, the breadth, the hugeness, the darkness of it that isn't really dark.

I realized that people think of grief as being dark and of darkness being bad. But actually, it's just like night. It's beautiful. The electricity of it is like a star-filled night. It's neither a bad experience nor a good one. It's just a different experience. I began to see how I was going to survive.

In the weeks that followed, I rode waves of feeling that threw me from one extreme to another. I'd be sobbing, then, moments later, I would be filled with ecstasy and gratitude at being able to see a sunrise, hear the sounds of morning, feel the warmth of a cup of tea in my hand.

Weeks passed, and then months. Today, as my heart continues to heal, I am more and more at peace. Sometimes I still feel angry. I did *not* want to lose the man I finally felt happy with. But I watch as emotions come and go, like a storm that blows in. It rains, the sun comes out, there's a rainbow. Another storm whips in, rips a tree out, then it's calm again.

People's lives and deaths, the appearances and exits in our lives, are in a sense not real. What feels real to me is the love, and that endures. When I lost Matthew, I felt smashed to bits, then discovered that what I really am cannot be destroyed. Knowing this, I can say that life has become deeper, more beautiful, more mysterious than I ever thought it could be.

Lindy Jones

Pause and Reflect

1. What practice(s) connects you with your source?
2. How do you create stillness for yourself, or how could you?
3. Sit quietly with your eyes closed. See if you can find an underlying silence, even in the midst of noise (both inner and outer).

LIFE LESSON #4:
DISCOVER THE MAGIC

....

Life is not measured by the number of breaths
we take, but by the moments
that take our breath away.

GEORGE CARLIN

The late Doug Henning and the word "magic" were synonymous. Doug once lived down the street from me. In fact, I attended his wedding to a beautiful woman named Debbie. It was a delightful and magical affair filled with beauty and love—and white doves appearing right out of the folds of Debbie's very full wedding dress, as the magician laughingly wove together the wondrous and the sacred.

Doug always seemed to be filled with wonder, and he loved to evoke it in others through his magic. One of the greatest magicians in history, he performed *The Magic Show* on Broadway for four years, then turned it into an annual TV spectacular, *The World of Magic,* which attracted millions of viewers. But he had almost forgotten why he became a magician when an amazing encounter reminded him.

While on tour, he was invited to do a show for a group of Inuits (Eskimos). He told the story of what happened in the following interview with *MAGIC, The Magazine for Magicians.* He was humbled by his experience with the Inuits and affected by the understanding they gave him of "magic" for the rest of his life.

Doug's experience helped me see things differently, too. After a visit to another country, for example, I breathe a sigh of relief to have hot running water available everywhere. I marvel at the choices I have in the grocery store. I am in awe of being able to have breakfast on the east coast and dinner on the west. I flip a switch and instantly I have air to cool or warm me. I can connect instantly with people all over the world through e-mail. Are these things not magic, too?

Earlier in this book, we looked at a life lesson to try something different. Why not just look at something differently, too—a friend, a convenience, a technology that makes life easier. Can you see the magic?

Real Magic

We were on the edge of this little town in the wilderness, 400 miles from the North Pole, and about 60 degrees below zero. I set up my show in a little building, and the Inuits came in to watch. They sat on the floor in their parkas, and I did what I thought was some pretty good stuff. They just sat there, didn't smile, didn't say a word and, at the end, nobody applauded. But they were completely focused on me, like I was some sort of phenomenon. Only one of them spoke English, so I asked him, "Did you like the show?"

"Yes, we like show," he said.

Then I asked, "Did everybody like the magic?"

He said, "The magic?"

I explained that I was trying to entertain people.

He said, "Entertainment is good, but why are you doing magic? The whole world is magical." We sat down on the floor and he told me, "It's magic that snow falls; all those little crystals are completely different. That's magic."

I said, "But what about when I made the rabbit and doves appear?"

"Why do you do those things?" he said. "It's magic when the walrus appears each spring; he comes from nowhere. That's magic."

Now I was grasping, trying to explain magic to him. I thought of my Zombie, which I thought was my best thing. I said, "I made that beautiful silver ball float in the air; that's magic."

"But there's a ball of fire floating through the sky every day. It keeps us warm, gives us light; that's magic."

Then the Inuits started talking among themselves. The man came to me with a big smile on his face, and said, "Now we know why you are doing that. It's because your people have forgotten the magic. You're doing it to remind them of the magic. Well done!"

I cried right then. I said, "Thank you for teaching me about the magic. I didn't know."

That was really the first time I knew what wonder was. It was the most memorable thing that has ever happened to me. I never forgot that, inside.

Doug Henning
as told to David Charvet for **MAGIC** **Magazine**

Pause and Reflect

1. Look around you. Find something you normally take for granted and ask yourself if it is not a wondrous thing. Whether it is the sun coming up, water flowing easily from a tap, or the fact that a coworker smiled at you for the first time, try to find the wonder in three "normal" things today.
2. Has anything extraordinary or out of the ordinary happened to you lately? Start to notice things like synchronicities and coincidences. For example, you think of someone and the phone rings—it's he or she calling.

LIFE LESSON #5:
GO BEYOND REASON

....

One cannot help but be in awe when
he contemplates the mysteries of eternity, of life,
of the marvelous structure of reality.

ALBERT EINSTEIN

My friend and I were leaving her parents' townhouse in New Orleans when we got held up because she couldn't find the key to lock it. She said, "I wonder what was on the road that we were meant to miss." It was the first time I had ever thought about delays and obstacles being blessings in disguise.

But didn't we hear hundreds of stories via email that confirmed this following 9/11, stories of people who should have been in the Twin Towers when they were destroyed—but weren't?

We read about the head of one company who arrived late that day because his son started kindergarten. Another man was alive because it was his turn to bring doughnuts to the office.

One woman was late because her alarm clock didn't go off in time. Another missed her bus. One's car wouldn't start. One couldn't get a taxi. Still another got stuck on the New Jersey Turnpike because of an accident.

One spilled food on her clothes and had to take time to

change. One went back to answer the telephone. One had a child who dawdled and didn't get ready as soon as he should have.

One man put on a new pair of shoes that morning and developed a blister on his foot before he got to work. He is alive today because he stopped at a drugstore to buy a Band-Aid.

The stories are endless, as they always are in times of disaster—and just as true in the opposite direction. While some people's lives are saved because of an unanticipated change to their routine, others undoubtedly lose their lives for the same reason.

For those who escape disaster with their lives, the feeling is always one of the miraculous, which is certainly true in the following story by Indian clothes designer Meenakshi Advani. Her story points out how sometimes we have to go beyond reason, beyond rational thought, to understand why things unfold the way they do. Like my New Orleans friend's comment indicated, there is likely to be a bigger picture. We may not be able to stand back in the midst of the situation to "get it" at the time, but hindsight will reveal that there was more to it than met the eye.

This understanding can help us to relax, knowing that we are always at the right place at the right time. A yoga teacher we know once noted that no one is ever "late" to her class; even if a student's not there when class begins, everyone arrives "on time"—for himself.

And have you ever noticed that, when asked "Why?" about something, you can't really answer? Sometimes you just have to say, "I don't know; it just doesn't feel right to me." In other words, you can't find the reason—but you know it doesn't matter.

Sometimes, it's just okay to go beyond reason.

🍵 Miracle in Mumbai

It was just another manic day at work. I was attending to all the regular chores at my clothing manufacturing business in Mumbai (formerly Bombay), India, prioritizing what needed to get done and formulating a back-up plan in case there were complications—which there often were. But this day went quite smoothly, so much so that at 6:00 in the evening, my entire staff of sixty-five was ready to leave. This is rare, as in the apparel manufacturing and designing industry there are always delays in everything. It is usually closer to 7:00 when we close down for the day.

We are a close-knit group. For many years I have trained my staff to do exquisite beading, painting, embroidering, sewing—everything required to manifest my unique and unusual clothing designs. Through the ups and downs of business, even in the toughest financial times, I have always tried to ensure that they were financially secure.

On this evening, I went around to each of my four divisions: office, showroom, embroidery, factory. After my final round at embroidery, where they were checking the pillow panels that were to be shipped the next day, I went to the factory. It was 6:05 PM, and they were all there with their backpacks, ready to leave.

I am not sure what compelled me to hold them back, in spite of their smiling, eager faces and their backpacks on their backs, signifying they were ready to rush out. But for some reason I felt the need to talk to them. First, I asked them for a detailed report of the day. Then I started speaking to them about preparations for the next day. As I was speaking, I was thinking to myself how nice it was that they were going home early for a change. I asked myself: *Why am I talking so much? I should just let them go. What I am saying can really wait until tomorrow. I need to let them go. Are they even listening to me?*

It was clear that they were getting antsy and a little irritated. Finally, at 6:20 PM, I let them off the hook. They were like a group of eager schoolkids who could hardly wait for the bell to ring. As I told them good-bye, they rushed out for the station, just a five-minute walk from my office.

Moments later, I was sitting in my car ready to leave, too, when I received a call from a friend. She told me there had been a huge bomb blast on one of the trains on the western railway line! At first my mind felt paralyzed. Then

I panicked. All I could think of were my sixty-five employees, most of whom traveled home on that local railway line.

I desperately tried making some calls, but all the phone lines were jammed. I tried to make sense of what had happened. A few of my employees had actually left at 6:05; were they on the train that had been bombed? (I would later learn that these were the handful of employees who lived close by and did not have to take the train to work.)

I sat trying to figure out the timing of everything that happened, but all I could be sure of was that some of them must have missed the bombed train. I suddenly realized, *If I hadn't kept them late, talking and going over plans, they might have been killed!* I felt deeply humbled, as if some guiding hand had used me to save them.

To my immense relief, at around 6:35 PM, I received a call from one of my staff members who told me that the one embroiderer who had left earlier than the others had heard that another train had just been bombed and stayed behind to stop all the remaining staff from getting on any of the later trains.

The next morning was bleak. We learned that several trains had been bombed in a matter of eleven minutes, starting at 6:24. More than 200 people had lost their lives; more than 700 had been wounded in the attacks. The devastation hit the city hard. Everyone seemed somber, uncertain of when all this terror would stop.

I was not expecting any of my employees to come to work that morning. But at 10:00 AM, I learned that every single one of my staff had come to work. Some had stayed overnight at friends' homes; others had come in on the same train line that had been bombed, which must have taken great courage. It seemed that in spite of the shock, the city was up and running.

I immediately got dressed and rushed off to be with them. I thanked them for coming, and I let them know how glad I was that they were safe.

But as I spoke, I saw fear and anguish in their eyes and noticed they seemed quiet and uncomfortable, and I knew why. In my company, I employ both Hindus and Muslims, men and women of different age groups. I realized that because of the terrorism, there was tension between the two religious groups.

I was determined to do something to overcome that tension. I had put years of effort into maintaining a "no discrimination" policy in my company. That is what made us very special. When we prayed as a company, at all our festivals and on other occasions, we honored both religions, Muslim and Hindu. The Hindus prayed with the Muslims, and the Muslims prayed with the Hindus!

So on this difficult day, I ordered a big, elaborate lunch for everyone. We all sat in the factory with plenty of food and cold soft drinks, and some music. Tension eased and hearts softened, as everyone began talking with one another. We all felt safe and blessed, and I said a prayer of thanks that not one of them had been on those doomed trains.

But the story did not end there. Several months later, while writing this story, my landlord doubled my rent, and I began to prepare to temporarily close my factory. I felt so concerned for these people who had become like family to me. I feared for their welfare, and I knew how difficult it would be personally to lose them.

Little did I know that they understood all this. As I sat in silence in my factory cabin, my people came to me one by one. They told me not to feel pressured, to take my time finding the right place. They assured me that they could take other jobs to survive for two or three months—but they would all be with me. As soon as I was ready, they would return.

I asked them, "What if you like your new work better?"

They simply smiled and replied, "We'll be back—guaranteed!" I could not stop crying. I realized they were there for me and that was enough.

Who knows what the future holds? I will do everything I can to get my business back on track as quickly as possible. But I have truly learned from these beautiful, humble people what gratitude and loyalty mean. My life will be forever imprinted by them.

Meenakshi Advani

Pause and Reflect

1. The next time someone asks you "Why?" don't try to come up with a logical answer if it doesn't come to you right away. See if "It just feels right" (or the opposite) is enough of a reason for feeling the way you do.

2. The next time you ask someone "Why?"—even a child—notice if they have trouble coming up with an answer. If so, consider cutting them a little slack, knowing that the "reason" may just be a feeling that can't be explained.

LIFE LESSON #6:
GIVE THANKS FOR MOMENTS OF MYSTERY

Precisely the least, the softest, lightest, a lizard's
rustling, a breath, a breeze, a moment's glance—
it is the little that makes the best happiness.

FRIEDRICH NIETZSCHE

I kept wondering why I wanted to share the next story with you, my own. Then one day I picked up *O* magazine and read an article by Krista Tippett, who gave me the perfect language for my experience.

She said that "the ancient Celts spoke of 'thin places' and 'thin times'—when the veil between heaven and earth is worn thin, where the temporal and the transcendent seem to touch." Moments of mystery, she called them. Like all the other stories in this chapter, this one is about one of those moments.[1]

But the point is this: life happens. Sometimes it's great, sometimes not so great. Sometimes it's filled with pain; sometimes, pleasure. At times we can find a deeper meaning; at others, nothing seems to make sense. The same act of God that saves one life causes another's pain or death.

What is this mystery? It is bigger than we can imagine. Just look at photos taken by the Hubble telescope of our galaxy and beyond, and you'll realize that we are the smallest of the small, and yet gifted with so much. If you're lucky enough to have money to pay your bills and the luxury of buying a book like this one, you are blessed. Even so, look beyond the material to the abundance of love, friendship, comfort, and wisdom so many of us have been gifted with. Don't try to figure it out: it's unfathomable.

And in the end, it doesn't really matter so much what we call the "life lesson" here, only that we acknowledge these moments and happenings for what they are and pause long enough to say thank you to the universe and the divine hand that guides it.

A Personally Recorded Message

My biological father was killed six weeks before I was born. He was riding home on his moped from his job at the huge Exxon refinery in Baton Rouge when he was hit by a truck driver who ran a red light. He died instantly.

I grew up close to my grandparents and uncles on his side of the family. I loved looking at the photo of him and his two younger brothers at my grandparents'; I looked just like him. I often asked my mother questions about him, and through the years, enjoyed receiving mementos of him and my parents' brief, eleven-month marriage: my mother's engagement ring, which they had had made in Budapest, where they met; a newspaper photo of their wedding in England; silver candelabras given to them as a wedding gift by a Russian colonel.

A few weeks before Christmas 2006, I was thinking of him, as I often do around the anniversary of his death. It's usually a fleeting acknowledgement of the day, but on this day, it was accompanied by a momentary longing as I sighed and thought, for the first time ever, *I wish I could have heard his voice.* Then I quickly let it go.

The day after Christmas an envelope arrived from my uncle. I noticed immediately that it was smaller than usual; for years this uncle's annual holiday gift had been a print of one of his commercial paintings of Louisiana landscapes. I couldn't imagine the reason for such a change of habit.

As I opened it, I felt a sense of intrigue and mystery. Inside the package were a CD and an envelope on which a note written in red in my uncle's handwriting announced: "STOP!! Open ONLY AFTER playing the CD!!"

Now I was really curious. I took the CD out of its case and pressed play. I heard what sounded like a very old, scratchy record with men's voices singing "I've Been Working on the Railroad." I stood in my living room thinking, *What? Why in the world is Uncle Bill sending me a recording of . . .* I stopped mid thought. *Oh, my goodness, one of those voices is my father's!* I burst into tears. Then I thought, *But how will I ever know which voice is his?*

I tore open the envelope and found this note:

> *This CD was transferred and cleaned from a small 45 rpm recording made in 1945 at a USO in Indianapolis. The quartet is composed of 18-year-old soldiers stationed at Ft. Campbell, Ky. The lead melody part is sung by L. N. Stracener, Jr., who had an excellent baritone voice (he sang some student operas at LSU). I hope you will find this as fascinating as I did! Uncle Bill*

I had my answer. I played the songs (there were two) over and over again, easily picking out my father's voice. In fact, since then I have memorized his voice and can recall it in my mind any time I want to.

One more thing was enclosed in the envelope: a photo-copy of the original envelope in which the record had been mailed. The date stamp on the envelope showed it was mailed from Indianapolis, December 3, 1945. He would meet my mother the following year and marry her the next December; I was born the following December, two years after the recording was made.

On the right side, the envelope was addressed to my father in his own hand to his family's address in Baton Rouge. On the left was a drawing of a record with the word "Recordio-Gram" printed across it.

I got chills as, below that, I read: "A Personally Recorded Message for You." It had taken sixty-one years to reach me, but it arrived only seven weeks after I had wished for it. The unfathomable mystery of the universe was at work, and I, its eternally grateful recipient.

Jennifer Read Hawthorne

Pause and Reflect

Practice giving thanks. For the next week, after you get into bed at night, try to find five things that happened that day to be thankful for.

Notes

ESSENTIAL INGREDIENT #2: LIFE LESSON #2
1. Chopra, Deepak. (1991) *Unconditional Life.* Bantam Books.

ESSENTIAL INGREDIENT #2: LIFE LESSON #3
1. Roth, Gabrielle. (1997) *Sweat Your Prayers.* Jeremy P. Tarcher/Putnam.
2. See www.walking.about.com.

ESSENTIAL INGREDIENT #2: LIFE LESSON #4
1. Schaef, Anne Wilson. (1987) *When Society Becomes an Addict.* Harper & Row.

ESSENTIAL INGREDIENT #2: LIFE LESSON #5
1. Begley, Sharon. (2007) *Train Your Mind, Change Your Brain.* Ballantine Books.
2. Pokea, Dr. Darryl. "Whose Thought Is It Anyway?" www.drpokea.com.

ESSENTIAL INGREDIENT #3: LIFE LESSON #5
1. Tourles, Stephanie. (2001). *How to Feel Fabulous Today.* Adapted by www.care2.com/greenliving/sleep.
2. "Ithaca," C. P. Cavafy, translated by George Barbanis. See users.hol.gr/~barbanis/.

ESSENTIAL INGREDIENT #4: LIFE LESSON #1
1. Dyer, Wayne. PBS television special *The Power of Intention.*

ESSENTIAL INGREDIENT #4: LIFE LESSON #2

1. Edwards, Jaroldeen Asplund and Anne Marie Oborn (illustrator). (2004) *The Daffodil Principle.* Shadow Mountain.

ESSENTIAL INGREDIENT #4: LIFE LESSON #4

1. Shwartz, Mark. "People from distant lands have strikingly similar genetic traits, study reveals." *Stanford Report* (January 8, 2003).

ESSENTIAL INGREDIENT #5: LIFE LESSON #1

1. Brothers, Dr. Joyce. (1988) *Dr. Joyce Brothers' The Successful Woman.* Simon & Shuster Adult Publishing Group.
2. Kogan, Lisa. "Q & O: Turn the Table." *O Magazine's 20th Anniversary Celebration! About Oprah.* October 2005.
3. Borysenko, Joan. (1999) *A Woman's Journey to God.* Riverhead Books.

ESSENTIAL INGREDIENT #5: LIFE LESSON #2

1. Darrach, Brad. "A Different Kind of Superstar." *Life* magazine (December 1995).
2. Kaminski, Patricia and Richard Katz. (1994) *Flower Essence Repertory.* The Flower Essence Society.

ESSENTIAL INGREDIENT #5: LIFE LESSON #4

1. Twist, Lynne. (2003) *The Soul of Money.* W.W. Norton.
2. U.S. Census Bureau Report (2000).
3. Sieloff, Sarah. "A Responsibility to the Poor." www.eckerd.edu.
4. Wise, Nina. (2002) *A Big New Free Happy Unusual Life.* Broadway Books.

ESSENTIAL INGREDIENT #6: LIFE LESSON #1

1. Mandela, Nelson. (1996) *Nelson Mandela: An Illustrated Autobiography.* Little, Brown and Company.

2. Ponder, Catherine. (1963) *The Dynamic Laws of Prosperity.* Prentice-Hall, Inc.

3. Cool, Lisa Collier. "The Power of Forgiving." *Reader's Digest,* May 2004.

ESSENTIAL INGREDIENT #6: LIFE LESSON #4

1. Len, Ihaleakala Hew, Ph.D. and Charles Brown, LMT. (1999) "Self-Identity Through Ho'oponopono." www.hooponopono.org.

ESSENTIAL INGREDIENT #7: LIFE LESSON #6

1. Tippett, Krista. "Something to Think About/The Soul Checkup." *O Magazine.* May 2007.

More Chicken Soup

Many of the stories and poems you have read in this book were submitted by readers like you who had read earlier Chicken Soup for the Soul books. We publish many Chicken Soup for the Soul books every year. We invite you to contribute a story to one of these future volumes.

Stories may be up to 1,200 words and must uplift or inspire. You may submit an original piece, something you have read, or your favorite quotation on your refrigerator door.

To obtain a copy of our submission guidelines and a listing of upcoming *Chicken Soup* books, please write, fax, or check our website.

Please send your submissions to:

Website: *www.chickensoup.com*
Chicken Soup for the Soul
P.O. Box 30880
Santa Barbara, CA 93130
Fax: 805-563-2945

Just send a copy of your stories and other pieces to the above address.

We will be sure that both you and the author are credited for your submission.

For information about speaking engagements, other books, audiotapes, workshops, and training programs, please contact any of our authors directly.

Supporting Others

In the spirit of supporting others, a portion of the proceeds from *Life Lessons for Loving the Way You Live* will be donated to North Star Dimensions, Inc.

North Star Dimensions is a non-profit (501-3C) educational and research organization founded in 1986 for the purpose of creating a vision for personal and planetary healing and the development of human potential. The group:

- develops methodologies and training for accelerated learning, peak performance, and higher states of well being
- offers education and training in multiple anti-aging methodologies that promote regeneration and longevity
- researches the use of sound and the development of music therapies for healing and elevating human insight and awareness

Lectures, workshops, and consulting are offered around the globe. For more information on programs and services, please contact:

North Star Dimensions, Inc.
c/o James A. Thompson, CPA
6122 Yellowood Road
Charlotte, NC 28210
phone: 641-472-8830
e-mail: northstardimensions@gmail.com

Who Is Jack Canfield?

Jack Canfield is the cocreator and editor of the Chicken Soup for the Soul series, which *Time* magazine has called "the publishing phenomenon of the decade." The series includes more than 140 titles with over 100 million copies in print in forty-seven languages. Jack is also the coauthor of eight other best-selling books, including *The Success Principles™: How to Get from Where You Are to Where You Want to Be, Dare to Win, The Aladdin Factor, You've Got to Read This Book,* and *The Power of Focus: How to Hit Your Business, Personal and Financial Targets with Absolute Certainty.*

Jack has recently developed a telephone coaching program and an online coaching program based on his most recent book, *The Success Principles.* He also offers a seven-day Breakthrough to Success seminar every summer, which attracts 400 people from about fifteen countries around the world.

Jack is the CEO of Chicken Soup for the Soul Enterprises and the Canfield Training Group in Santa Barbara, California, and is founder of the Foundation for Self-Esteem in Culver City, California. He has conducted intensive personal and professional development seminars on the principles of success for more than a million people in twenty-nine countries around the world. Jack is a dynamic keynote speaker, and he has spoken to hundreds of thousands of others at more than 1,000 corporations, universities, professional conferences, and conventions and has been seen by millions more on national television shows such as *Oprah, Montel, The Today Show, Larry King Live, Fox and Friends, Inside Edition, Hard Copy,* CNN's *Talk Back Live, 20/20, Eye to Eye,* and the *NBC Nightly News* and the *CBS Evening News.* Jack was also a featured teacher in the hit movie *The Secret.*

Jack is the recipient of many awards and honors, including three honorary doctorates and a Guinness World Records Certificate for having seven books from the Chicken Soup for the Soul series appearing on the *New York Times* bestseller list on May 24, 1998.

To write to Jack or for inquiries about Jack as a speaker, his coaching programs, trainings, or seminars, use the following contact information:

Jack Canfield
The Canfield Companies
P.O. Box 30880 • Santa Barbara, CA 93130
phone: 805-563-2935 • fax: 805-563-2945
E-mail: info4jack@jackcanfield.com
www.jackcanfield.com

Who Is Mark Victor Hansen?

In the area of human potential, no one is more respected than Mark Victor Hansen. For more than thirty years, Mark has focused solely on helping people from all walks of life reshape their personal vision of what's possible. His powerful messages of possibility, opportunity, and action have created powerful change in thousands of organizations and millions of individuals worldwide.

He is a sought-after keynote speaker, bestselling author, and marketing maven. Mark's credentials include a lifetime of entrepreneurial success and an extensive academic background. He is a prolific writer with many bestselling books, such as *The One Minute Millionaire, Cracking the Millionaire Code, How to Make the Rest of Your Life the Best of Your Life, The Power of Focus, The Aladdin Factor,* and *Dare to Win,* in addition to the Chicken Soup for the Soul series. Mark has made a profound influence through his library of audios, videos, and articles in the areas of big thinking, sales achievement, wealth building, publishing success, and personal and professional development.

Mark is the founder of the MEGA Seminar Series. MEGA Book Marketing University and Building Your MEGA Speaking Empire are annual conferences where Mark coaches and teaches new and aspiring authors, speakers, and experts on building lucrative publishing and speaking careers. Other MEGA events include MEGA Info-Marketing and My MEGA Life.

As a philanthropist and humanitarian, Mark works tirelessly for organizations such as Habitat for Humanity, American Red Cross, March of Dimes, Childhelp USA, and many others. He is the recipient of numerous awards that honor his entrepreneurial spirit, philanthropic heart, and business acumen. He is a lifetime member of the Horatio Alger Association of Distinguished Americans, an organization that honored Mark with the prestigious Horatio Alger Award for his extraordinary life achievements.

Mark Victor Hansen is an enthusiastic crusader of what's possible and is driven to make the world a better place.

Mark Victor Hansen & Associates, Inc.
P.O. Box 7665 • Newport Beach, CA 92658
phone: 949-764-2640 • fax: 949-722-6912
www.markvictorhansen.com

Who Is Jennifer Read Hawthorne?

Jennifer Read Hawthorne is coauthor of the #1 *New York Times* best-sellers *Chicken Soup for the Woman's Soul* and *Chicken Soup for the Mother's Soul.* An inspirational writer, speaker, and educator, she has a passion for exploring consciousness and the development of human potential. Her personal quest for peace and transformation has taken her around the world and provided a lifetime of rich experiences, from Baton Rouge to Kathmandu, from Mother Teresa to the Masai.

Known as a dynamic and insightful speaker, Jennifer learned the art of storytelling as a child in her native Louisiana from her father, a journalist and master storyteller whose original Brer Rabbit stories filled her childhood with magic and a sense of the power of words. Later, as a Peace Corps volunteer in West Africa, she rediscovered the universality of stories to teach, move, uplift, and connect people. With humor, wisdom, and a multicultural view of life, she offers her audiences powerful and effective ways to find greater meaning, authenticity, and personal power.

Jennifer's award-winning writing spans the full range from technical software manuals to poetry—and numerous books in between. In addition to the bestsellers listed above, her books include *A Second Chicken Soup for the Woman's Soul; Chicken Soup for the Single's Soul; The Soul of Success: A Woman's Guide to Authentic Power;* and *Diamonds, Pearls & Stones: Jewels of Wisdom for Young Women.* Her books have sold more than 13 million copies and have been translated into more than thirty languages.

Jennifer has appeared on CNN, *Pure Oxygen, Sally Jesse Raphael,* and hundreds of national, regional, and local television and radio shows. She has been featured in numerous magazine and newspaper articles, and has written articles for national magazines such as *Entrepreneur* and *Ladies Home Journal.* She holds a degree in journalism and is a regular columnist for *Affluent* magazine.

Recently, Jennifer has begun exploring cutting-edge methods and technologies for super-learning, regeneration, and the expansion of consciousness. A lover of yoga, she passionately believes that her greatest contribution to the world is to be at peace herself. She feels that loving life whatever its circumstances is her greatest achievement and blessing.

For more information or to book Jennifer for a keynote presentation or private consulting, visit her website: www.jenniferhawthorne.com.

Contributors

Meenakshi Advani is an international fashion designer whose collection can be found in the U.S. under the Dancing Peacock label. A former Miss Dubai and fashion model, she has lived and worked in the U.S., but currently resides in her home city of Mumbai, India. She practices social empowerment with great passion at her studio, factory, and embroidery workshop in Mumbai, by hiring, nurturing, and training underprivileged men and women and motivating them to create world-class hand-crafted couture and upscale apparel, home furnishings, and fashion accessories, which she exports around the world. Contact her at dancingpeacock@rosemooninc.com or visit her website www.rosemooninc.com.

Angeles Arrien is president of the Foundation for Cross-Cultural Education and Research. She lectures and conducts workshops worldwide, bridging cultural anthropology, psychology, and comparative religions. Ms. Arrien's work is currently used in medical, academic, and corporate environments. Her books, including *The Four-Fold Way, The Signs of Life*, and *The Second Half of Life*, have been translated into nine languages, and she has received three honorary degrees in recognition of her work.

Janet Bray Attwood is the coauthor of the number-one national bestseller, *The Passion Test: The Effortless Path to Discovering Your Destiny* (www.thepassiontest.com), and the cofounder of the online transformational magazine, *Healthy Wealthy nWise* (www.healthywealthynwise.com), where she interviews famous leaders on what it means to live a passionate life. Janet has presented her programs as a featured speaker to thousands of people all over the world. For more about Janet go to www.janetattwood.com.

Nancy Bellmer lives for the inner experience of life more than the outer. She is a wife and mother who enjoys meditating, teaching, making pottery, giving massage, exploring nature, and sharing loving relationships with friends and family. She offers her story with the hope readers will gain healing and expansion.

Chellie Campbell created the popular Financial Stress Reduction Workshop and is the author of two books on making more money and having more time off for fun: *The Wealthy Spirit* and *Zero to Zillionaire.* She is a professional speaker, seminar leader, poker champion, and author, and has been prominently quoted as a financial expert in the *Los Angeles Times, Pink, Good Housekeeping, Essence, Woman's World* magazines, Lifetime TV network, and more than fifteen popular books. For more information on her workshops, speaking engagements, books, free e-zine, and to join the Dolphin Club, visit www.chellie.com or contact her at Chellie@chellie.com.

Linda Chaé is president and chief formulator for Chaé Organics, Inc. and a pioneer in "go natural" skin care for consumers. Her commitment to clean, safe, toxin-free products requires organic ingredients backed by scientific research (see www.toxicfree.org). Protecting human beings from dangers in skin-care products became a personal crusade when she became a cancer survivor herself (see www.lindachae.com.) To order her products, visit www.chaecorp.com. To book Linda as a speaker, call 719-742-5288, or send a request via e-mail to pr@chaecorp.com.

Lane Hawley Cole loaded up her car and motored out of the frigid Midwest. She landed (if it's possible to land a sedan) in southwest Florida. Lane hasn't ridden much since she was seventeen but fondly remembers a lesson horse named Trigger. One day she hopes to go on a mountain trail ride with a horse like Trigger. Tennis is now Lane's passion and clay court singles is her favorite pastime.

Dr. Paul Dunion has been in private practice as a psychotherapist and is a writer. He leads a variety of workshops that have been offered on a national level. Dr. Dunion's most notable work is in the area of relationship and intimacy. In September of 2004 he published his first book, *Temptation in the House of the Lord,* and has published a dozen articles related to family life. In 2006 he published his second book, *Shadow Marriage: A Descent into Intimacy.* You can contact Paul at www.PaulDunion.com.

Vicky Edmonds is a poet and teacher who uses the art and practice of writing to help people bring their most authentic voice to the page and to the world. Her published works include five books of poetry and two books of writing exercises, and she is currently working on her forthcoming book, *One Cell in the Body of God: Poetry as a Therapeutic & Spiritual Practice.* For more information, call 206-937-0700, or visit www.ealloftheabove.com.

Linda Elliott spent fifteen years with Visa International. As executive vice president she managed the technology that makes Visa cards work globally and created new systems for electronic commerce. Later, she served as president of the PingID Network, where she focused on frictionless, secure electronic interactions. Today, Linda is a partner in Glenbrook Partners, a management consulting firm. Linda also mentors and serves on a number of corporate boards.

Pamela George, Ph.D., recently opened her painting studio in Durham, North Carolina, after serving as an educational psychology professor for three decades. While work assignments with the Peace Corps and the Fulbright program have led her to exotic places—Samoa, Portugal, China, and Southeast Asia—she always comes home to her native South. George's paintings and contact information can be found at www.pamelageorge.net.

Leah Green, founder and director of The Compassionate Listening Project, holds masters degrees in public policy and Middle Eastern studies from the University of Washington. Leah is an internationally recognized facilitator and trainer. She has led twenty-one training delegations to Israel/Palestine, produced three documentaries about the conflict, and cofounded Jewish-German Compassionate Listening. Leah is a recipient of the *Yoga Journal's* Karma Yoga Award, and she teaches Compassionate Listening world wide. For more information, visit: www.compassionatelistening.org.

Ellen Greene received her Ph.D. from Berkeley in 1992. She is a professor of classics at the University of Oklahoma and specializes in the study of women and sexuality in ancient Greek and Latin love poetry. Her books include *Reading Sappho; The Erotics of Domination: Male Desire and the Mistress in Latin Love Poetry; Gendered Dynamics in Latin Love Poetry:* and *Women Poets in Greece and Rome.*

Elinor Daily Hall is the project manager for the Center for Soulful Living, an organization dedicated to personal transformation and growth. Her supportive role in CSL has been pivotal in the expansion of the community and has served her personal quest for truth and empowerment. Elinor has had a rich professional life as an educator, businesswoman, and editor and is now relishing her newfound freedom, friends, and mission. Contact Elinor at elinor@aboutcsl.com.

Christine Horner, M.D. is a board-certified plastic surgeon with a special interest in natural medicine. She was honored by *Glamour* magazine and by Oprah after spearheading breast reconstruction legislation. Dr. Horner is the author of *Waking the Warrior Goddess: Dr. Christine Horner's Program to Protect Against and Fight Breast Cancer.*

Ciella Kollander is an international gold-record recording artist, composer, and teacher. She is currently writing her autobiography, *Bad Girl Yogi, Confessions of a Rascal on the Path,* producing her WholeBodySinging™ seminar video, and hoping to complete her CD with the great Roger Kellaway this year. Her short stories, articles, and poetry are becoming widely published. She can be reached via e-mail at ciellathewriter@yahoo.com.

Colin Mallard is the author of four books grounded in philosophical and spiritual understanding. *Uncommon Reason* offers insights into contemporary society's struggle with governing, war, and peace. *Something to Ponder* presents a contemporary version of Lao-tzu's *Tao Te Ching. The Examined Life* invites a deep, easily accessible exploration of spiritual awakening. The aforementioned books are published by Sat Nam Imprints, an imprint of Word Keepers, Inc. in Fort Collins, Colorado. His website is www.colinmallard.com.

Mackey McNeill is president/CEO of Mackey Advisors, a wealth management and CPA firm serving clients with prosperity planning, investment management, tax consulting, and business consulting services since 1983. As a CPA, personal financial specialist, investment advisor representative, and certified Enneagram teacher, Mackey supports her clients in expanding their prosperity. These ideas are captured in her award-winning book *The Intersection of Joy and Money.* Contact Mackey at Mackey@CultivatingProsperity.com and visit her website: www.CultivatingProsperity.com.

Michael Murphy has been a nursing assistant, a meditation teacher, a school teacher, a repairman, a carpenter, and a writing instructor. His book, *Murphy's Laws of the Inner Life*, documents his adventures and the lessons learned from them. In his seminar, Writing as a Sacred Practice, he teaches his students how to use writing as a tool for self-discovery. He can be reached by e-mail at michael@dawnhawk.com or through his website: www.dawnhawk.com.

Sara O'Meara and **Yvonne Fedderson** are the founders of Childhelp USA, which serves thousands of children daily with many comprehensive services, including the National Child Abuse Hotline, 800-4-A-CHILD. With the support of many kind humanitarians, they have opened several "villages" (residential treatment facilities) around the country for abused children, including one at an Arizona resort donated by Merv Griffin. To get help, call the hotline above. To give help, contact Childhelp at their national headquarters at 480-922-8212, or visit the website: www.childhelp.org.

Yaniyah Pearson, M.A., has been working with young people since 1981 and conducts national leadership development workshops. She spent three summers touring with African American, Latino, Asian American, and Native American young leaders throughout Russia and Uzbekistan. After twelve years with YouthBuild she now serves as a consultant to youth development organizations. Yaniyah is currently writing a novel, *Wind Island*, and a nonfiction work based on spiritual development for youth workers titled *Working with the Sacred*, from which "The Beat" is excerpted. She lives in the mid-Hudson Valley of New York State with her life partner.

Staci Ann Richmond is a mother, special education teacher, and freelance writer. She and her fiancé, Roger Wright, are collectively attempting to raise six children. A former newspaper reporter, Staci was named first place Master Columnist by the Iowa Newspaper Association and the Associated Press in 2003. Her work also appears in *Chicken Soup for the Mother's Soul II*. She can be reached by e-mail at staci.richmond@yahoo.com.

Meryl Runion, CSP (Certified Speaking Professional), helps people find the perfect words to say what they mean and get what they want. Her four books about Power Phrases have been translated into five languages and sold over 250,000 copies worldwide. Clients include IBM, which found her to be systematic; the IRS, which particularly loves her in April; and the FBI, which finds her to be a person of interest. Visit her website and subscribe to her free newsletter at www.speakstrong.com.

Stephen Shapiro began his diverse career with a fifteen-year tenure with the international consulting firm Accenture, where he founded and led their Global Process Excellence Practice. In 2001, he left the management consulting world to write his first book, *24/7 Innovation*, which has been heralded in *Newsweek, Investor's Business Daily*, and the *New York Times*. His most recent book, *Goal-Free Living* was the cover story in *O Magazine* and was featured in *Entrepreneur Magazine*. See www.goalfree.com or e-mail steve@goalfree.com.

Susan Brandis Slavin has been acting in film, TV, and theatre to critical acclaim and has won many awards since her early teens. She wrote and performed the successful one-woman play *Motherlove* and has been credited with innovating that popular genre of the one-person play. She founded Susan Slavin Actors and Singers Academy at Carnegie Hall, dedicated to personal transformation, creative mastery, and making professional dreams a reality. She is a director, designer, and producer as well. Recent highlights include costarring in a film shot on location in Greece and performing her autobiographical new play Off Broadway, now in development as an inspirational feature film. She may be contacted at 212-330-8798 or e-mail susanbrandisslavin@yahoo.com.

Rotarian **Dr. Ali Tahiri** is a passionate environmentalist and humanitarian who works toward integrating all modalities of medicine. He cofounded Wave Aid following the Asian tsunami with the students of Pine View School in Osprey, Florida. He recently received the 2006 and 2007 Humanitarian Awards from Operation Serving Children and the Global Foundation for Integrative Medicine respectively. He is a dynamic speaker who has spoken in many countries, motivating and inspiring many. Contact him at P.O. Box 19902, Sarasota, FL 34276. His e-mail is coo@naturalipro.com. Call him at 941-356-4100. Relief work information can be viewed at http://naturalipro.com/waveaid/mainpg.htm and www.gfim.info.

Lynne Twist is a global activist, fundraiser, author, and founder of the Soul of Money Institute. She has devoted her life to service in support of ending world hunger, global sustainability, human rights, economic integrity, and spiritual authenticity. Lynne has raised millions of dollars, and trained thousands of fundraisers to be more effective in their work for organizations that serve the best instincts of all of us: eradicating poverty, empowering women, nurturing children and youth, and preserving the natural heritage of our planet. Visit www.soulofmoney.org.

Born in New Rochelle, New York, **Virginia Whiting Walden** received her B.A. at Hiram College in 1969, then moved to Santa Fe, New Mexico, where she became a regionally known artist and performed flamenco and classical guitar. After cancer and Chi-Lel Qigong training in China, she relocated to Honolulu in 1999. Now about to publish her book *Cancer Gone!*, she is teaching Chi-Lel, creating art and music, and continuing to write. Contact Ginny at blueskyhealingarts@hawaii.rr.como, or call 808-259-8453. Her website is www.ginnywalden.com.

Over the past thirty-five years **Moorman Robertson Work Jr.** (Rob Work) has promoted human development in fifty-five countries around the world. His work has consisted of designing and implementing research, training, and demonstration projects in community, organizational, and leadership development. Rob served in leadership positions with a non-governmental organization, the Institute of Cultural Affairs, for twenty years and then as a chief policy advisor on decentralized governance with the United Nations Development Programme for fifteen years. He is now the founder/director of the Hillside Institute in Garrison, New York.

Permissions (*continued from page iv*)

The Global Citizen: A Love Story. Reprinted by permission of Moorman Robertson Work Jr. ©2007 Moorman Robertson Work Jr.

Olympic Heart. Reprinted by permission of Virigina Whiting Walden. ©2007 Virigina Whiting Walden.

Blurry Vision. Reprinted by permission of. ©2007 Mackey McNeill.

Due for a Change. Reprinted by permission of Staci Richmond. ©2007 Staci Richmond.

My Name Is Chellie C. Reprinted by permission of Chellie L. Campbell. ©2007 Chellie L. Campbell.

The Power of Choice. Reprinted by permission of Angeles Arrien. ©2007 Angeles Arrien.

Testing the Sleeping Giant. Reprinted by permission of Pamela George. ©2007 Pamela George.

The New York City Cab Driver. Reprinted by permission of Lynne Twist. ©2007 Lynne Twist.

Song of the Warrior Spirit. Reprinted by permission of Ciella Kollander. ©2007 Ciella Kollander.

Running with the Bulls. Reprinted by permission of Linda G. Elliott. ©2007 Linda G. Elliott.

My Odyssey. Reprinted by permission of Ellen Greene. ©2007 Ellen Greene.

Don't Take No for an Answer. Reprinted by permission of Ali Tahiri. ©2007 Ali Tahiri.

Somebody Should Do Something. Reprinted by permission of Vicky J. Edmonds. ©2007 Vicky J. Edmonds.

Finding Sarah. Reprinted by permission of Paul Dunion. ©2007 Paul Dunion.

The Secret Weapon. Reprinted by permission of Leah Green. ©2007 Leah Green.

Well of Strength. Adapted from "Sufficiency: The Surprising Truth," from *The Soul of Money: Transforming Your Relationship with Money and Life* by Lynne Twist.

Pursue your dreams

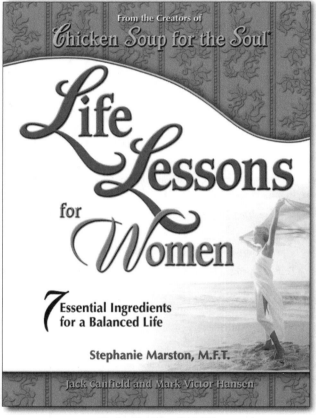

Code #1444 • $14.95

Each story in *Life Lessons for Women* will
touch your soul. And each will inspire you to make
every day—every minute—more fulfilling.

Organize your world

Code #5571 • $14.95

Discover this indispensable source of
encouragement to promote balance and a greater
quality of life for you and your family.

More in the series

Chicken Soup African American Soul
Chicken Soup African American Woman's Soul
Chicken Soup Breast Cancer Survivor's Soul
Chicken Soup Bride's Soul
Chicken Soup Caregiver's Soul
Chicken Soup Cat Lover's Soul
Chicken Soup Christian Family Soul
Chicken Soup College Soul
Chicken Soup Couple's Soul
Chicken Soup Dieter's Soul
Chicken Soup Dog Lover's Soul
Chicken Soup Entrepreneur's Soul
Chicken Soup Expectant Mother's Soul
Chicken Soup Father's Soul
Chicken Soup Fisherman's Soul
Chicken Soup Girlfriend's Soul
Chicken Soup Golden Soul
Chicken Soup Golfer's Soul, Vol. I, II
Chicken Soup Horse Lover's Soul, Vol. I, II
Chicken Soup Inspire a Woman's Soul
Chicken Soup Kid's Soul, Vol. I, II
Chicken Soup Mother's Soul, Vol. I, II
Chicken Soup Parent's Soul
Chicken Soup Pet Lover's Soul
Chicken Soup Preteen Soul, Vol. I, II
Chicken Soup Scrapbooker's Soul
Chicken Soup Sister's Soul, Vol. I, II
Chicken Soup Shopper's Soul
Chicken Soup Soul, Vol. I-VI
Chicken Soup at Work
Chicken Soup Sports Fan's Soul
Chicken Soup Teenage Soul, Vol. I-IV
Chicken Soup Woman's Soul, Vol. I, II

To order direct: Telephone (800) 441-5569 • www.hcibooks.com
Prices do not include shipping and handling. Your response code is CCS.